**A FIDELER/GATEWAY
STORY OF AMERICA BOOK**

GREAT AMERICANS

Mary Jane Fowler

&

Margaret Fisher

**Gateway
Press, Inc.**

Grand Rapids, Michigan

HISTORICAL ADVISOR

Clifton R. Fox
Department of History
Michigan State University

EDITORIAL AND DESIGN STAFF

Manuscript

Jerry E. Jennings
Tom Lee
Mary Mitus
Marion H. Smith

Art

Lee Brown
Ellen Osborn

Copyright 1988, Gateway Press, Inc.
Grand Rapids, Michigan
LIBRARY OF CONGRESS CATALOG CARD NUMBER: 87-081352
ISBN: 0-934291-25-X

Earlier Edition Copyright, The Fideler Company, 1968

Grateful acknowledgment is made to the following for permission to use the illustrations found in this book:

American Museum of Natural History, Department of Library Services: Page 119.
American Museum of Photography: Page 6.
American Red Cross: Pages 94 and 99.
Antioch College News Bureau: Page 93.
Barry Willis: Page 37.
The Beinecke Rare Book and Manuscript Library: Pages 142, 143, and 146.
The Bettmann Archive: Pages 36 and 148; page 67, courtesy of the Franklin D. Roosevelt Library.
Bowdoin College Museum of Fine Arts: Page 24.
The Brooklyn Museum: Page 45, painting by Eastman Johnson.
Brown Brothers: Pages 35, 40, 55, and 57.
Chicago Historical Society: Page 28.
City Art Museum of St. Louis: Page 90.
Country Beautiful: Page 23, painting by David Martin with permission from the Washington Historical Society.
Culver Pictures: Page 60.
Cushing: Pages 14, 114, 123, and 126.
Devaney: Pages 29, 30, and 124.
Diane Bartnick: Pages 59 and 61.
European Picture Service: Pages 106 and 120.
The Fideler Company: Pages 9, 25, 95, 97, 98, 107, 116, and 122.
Flip Schulke, "King Remembered": Page 81.
Ford Motor Company: Pages 121, 127, 128, 129, 130, 131, and 132.
Franklin D. Roosevelt Library: Pages 64, 66, 69, 70, and 74.
Franklin Technical Institute: Pages 15, 18, 19, 20, 21, and 22.
Fraunces Tavern Museum, Sons of the Revolution in the State of New York: Pages 11 and 12.
Freelance Photographers Guild: Page 63; page 88 by Fletcher Drake.
Galloway: Pages 7, 89, 100, and 112.
Gendreau: Page 31.
Donated by George Washington Carver National Monument, Diamond, Missouri: Pages 133 and 135.
Hendricks-Long Publishing Company, Dallas: Page 42.
Historical Pictures Service: Pages 51 and 153; page 48, painting by Henry H. Cross.
Hull House Association: Pages 103 and 105.
Jane Addams Memorial Collection, The University Library, University of Illinois at Chicago: Pages 102 and 104.
Painting by J. N. Marchand: Page 53.

John Hancock Mutual Life Insurance Company: Page 92.
Johnson Publishing Company: Pages 76-77, 78, 83, and 85.
Keystone View Company: Page 65.
Lee Brown: Cover, adapted from a painting by John Ward Dunsmore.
Library of Congress: Pages 17 and 41.
Lincoln National Life Foundation: Pages 32 and 33.
March of Dimes Birth Defects Foundation: Pages 149, 150, and 151.
Mark Twain Memorial, Hartford, CT: Page 113.
Martin Luther King, Jr., Center for Nonviolent Social Change, Inc.: Page 75.
Massie-Missouri Resources Division: Page 111.
Montana Historical Society: Page 54.
Museum of Modern Art: Page 109.
National Audubon Society: Pages 115 and 118.
Courtesy of the Newberry Library, Chicago: Page 46.
Photoreporters: Page 87.
P.H. Polk, Tuskegee, Alabama: Page 137.
Rachel Carson Council, Inc.: Page 141 by Erick Hartmann; pages 145 and 147 by Shirley Briggs.
Rinehart-Marsden, Inc.: Page 34.
Roberts: Page 101.
Smithsonian Institution: Page 26.
Sophia Smith Collection, Smith College: Page 62.
Thomas Gilcrease Institute of American History and Art: Page 52, painting by Olaf Seltzer.
Tuskegee Institute, National Historic Site, Tuskegee, Alabama: Pages 136 and 139.
Underwood and Underwood: Page 39.
United Press International: Pages 68, 84, and 86.
United States Capitol Historical Society: Page 38 by George F. Mobley.
United States Department of Commerce, Bureau of Public Roads: Page 49.
United States Department of the Interior, National Park Service, Edison National Historic Site: Page 125.
United States Department of the Interior, National Park Service, Springfield, VA: Page 140.
Virginia Museum of Fine Arts: Page 10; page 13, painting by J.B. Stearns.
The White House: Page 154.
Wide World Photos: Pages 73 (top) and 82; pages 72 and 73 (bottom) courtesy of the Franklin D. Roosevelt Library.

CONTENTS

George Washington was our first president. He is often called "The Father of His Country."

Chapter 1
George Washington
1732-1799

The hot June sun beat down on a disorderly column of retreating soldiers. Shouts filled the dusty, summer air. Neither the officers nor the commanding general were making any attempt to rally the fleeing army. Each man was looking out for himself. Suddenly, a white horse bearing a tall rider galloped to the crest of the hill toward which the men were running.

"It's General Washington!" shouted one soldier. The news flashed back from man to man. As if by magic, the troops halted and the noise died down. Quietly, the soldiers turned back to face the

*See Glossary

Washington was commander in chief of the colonial army during the Revolutionary War.* He helped the colonies win their independence.

enemy. Once again, George Washington had held the American army together. As in the past, his leadership had brought his country one step closer to winning the Revolutionary War.*

People who knew young George Washington never dreamed he would grow up to be a great leader. He was a shy boy who loved sports and games. Much of his time was spent riding horseback, hunting, or swimming near his father's Virginia estate. However, this quiet, athletic boy was sensible, dependable, and hardworking. Perhaps these were the qualities that caused people to like him, and made them feel that they could trust him.

One person who was especially fond of George was his oldest half brother, Lawrence. After their father died, when George was eleven, Lawrence tried to be like a father to his younger brother. He invited George to live with him at his home, "Mount Vernon." Here, George met many interesting, educated people. From them he learned good manners and social graces. Later, Lawrence hired two special teachers to instruct George in military skills, such as fencing and planning campaigns. The quiet, good manners and straight, military walk which Washington acquired during these years gave him a look of dignity that won people's respect.

Another man who liked and respected young Washington was a wealthy neighbor, Lord Thomas Fairfax. When the boy was only sixteen, Lord Fairfax thought he was dependable enough to help survey* some lands in the wilderness. George did his work so well that he was given the job of public surveyor. In this work, he learned much about life in the frontier forests. He also showed that he could withstand the hardships and discomforts of the wilderness.

Because of his wilderness experience and military training, Washington was asked to serve as an aide to General Braddock, the British commander in the French and Indian War.* During a terrible battle in the wilderness, General Braddock was wounded. His terrified soldiers were left completely at the mercy of the French and the Indians. Calmly, courageously, and forcefully, young Washington helped to rally the troops and lead them out of the wilderness. After this battle, people all over the colonies realized that George Washington was a leader on whom they could depend in an emergency.

Washington served as commander of all the Virginia troops for about three years. In 1759 he returned to Mount Vernon, which

Surveying* **land on the frontier.** In this work, Washington learned about life in the wilderness.

he had inherited from his half brother Lawrence. Here, he spent the days supervising the work on his large farms. With his wife, Martha, he enjoyed the company of many guests. Washington would have been happy to spend the rest of his life at Mount Vernon. However, when it later became clear that the Revolutionary War could not be avoided, he felt that he must leave his home to help his country in its fight for freedom.

Dressed in his military uniform, Washington joined the other colonial leaders who were attending the Second Continental Congress* in Philadelphia. The men around him remembered his courage and ability in the French and Indian War. They respected

Washington gained military experience as an officer during the French and Indian War.*

Washington and his family lived at Mount Vernon, which he had inherited from his half brother.

his quiet strength and devotion to his country. On June 15, 1775, they elected him commander in chief of the Continental Army.

Washington's job was very difficult. The soldiers under his command had almost no training. Some of his generals, who were jealous because he had been named commander in chief, plotted to overthrow him. Worst of all, the governments of the thirteen colonies did not work together to supply him with the food, clothing, and weapons he needed for his army.

The hardest months of the war came during the winter of 1777-1778, when Washington camped with his soldiers at Valley

At Valley Forge. Washington encouraged his ragged, hungry troops during the cold winter of 1777-1778.

Forge, in Pennsylvania. Cold winter winds whistled around the tiny log huts in which the troops had to live. The soldiers' clothes were too ragged and tattered to keep them warm. Many of them did not have shoes to wear. There was not enough food for them to eat. It is not surprising that some of the starving, freezing men became discouraged and went home. If it had not been for Washington, all of them might have left. Day after day, he rode through the camp, encouraging the troops. His strength and courage kept the tired little army together. In 1781, Washington led his army to final victory over the British.

Washington's leadership was still needed after the war was over. The thirteen states were not yet united into one strong nation. Some Americans thought this could best be done if George Washington would become dictator or king. Most men would have been glad to gain such power. Washington, however, was angry with the men who suggested this idea. He had fought hard for freedom. Now he worked hard to help Americans use their freedom wisely. He served as president of the group which wrote our democratic Constitution. Then he was elected to be the first president of the nation that he had helped to found. His leadership helped the American people to respect and support their new government. When we think of all that Washington did, it is not surprising that we call him "The Father of His Country."

Adopting the Constitution. Washington was president of the group which wrote our Constitution.

Benjamin Franklin was a great American statesman. He was also an author, scientist, and inventor.

Chapter 2
Benjamin Franklin
1706-1790

One summer afternoon about 275 years ago, young Ben Franklin ran down the stairs of his home in Boston, Massachusetts. Tucked under his arm were two wooden paddles about ten inches long and six inches wide, which he had just finished making.

14

"Where are you going?" called his mother, as he hurried out the door.

"Down to the pond to try an experiment," Ben answered.

When he reached the pond, Ben quickly undressed. Then he picked up a paddle in each hand and waded into the water. Soon he leaned forward and began to swim. The stiff paddles pushed strongly against the rippling water. They made his wrists tired, but he didn't care. The important thing was that they helped him to swim much faster, just as he had thought they would. His experiment was working!

Ben liked to perform experiments almost as much as he liked to read. In both reading and experimenting, he found answers to the many questions that always filled his mind. Surely there wasn't another boy in Boston so full of questions as young Ben Franklin.

Young Ben Franklin worked in his brother's print shop until he was seventeen years old.

Ben didn't have enough time for learning, because he had to spend his days earning a living. He was the fifteenth child in a family of seventeen. Though Mr. Franklin knew that young Ben had a keen, questioning mind, he could afford to send him to school for only about two years. After that, the boy had to go to work in the family candle shop. Cutting wicks and pouring wax was dull work for a bright boy like Ben. He became so restless and dissatisfied that Mr. Franklin was afraid he would run away and go to sea. Therefore, when Ben was twelve, he was put to work as an apprentice* in his brother James' printing shop.

There was more opportunity to learn in the print shop than in the candle shop, and Ben was much happier. He read and thought about the articles which he helped to print in his brother's newspaper. Then he wrote some articles of his own. Ben knew that James would not print these if he discovered that his younger brother was the author. Therefore, he signed them "Mrs. Silence Dogood," and slipped them under the door of the print shop at night. James thought the mysterious articles were excellent and printed them. However, he was furious when he finally found out who the real author was.

Ben had too many ideas of his own to be happy working for someone else. When he was seventeen, he ran away from Boston and went to Philadelphia. Though he had scarcely a penny to his name, young Franklin possessed more important riches. He had a good, questioning mind, and he dared to try out his ideas. By the time he was twenty-four, he had a print shop of his own.

Although Franklin had the most successful print shop in Philadelphia, he was interested in much more than business. For one thing, he liked to write. Each year, for twenty-five years, he wrote and published a book called *Poor Richard's Almanac*. Like other

*See Glossary

A page from *Poor Richard's Almanac*. Franklin published an almanac every year for twenty-five years.

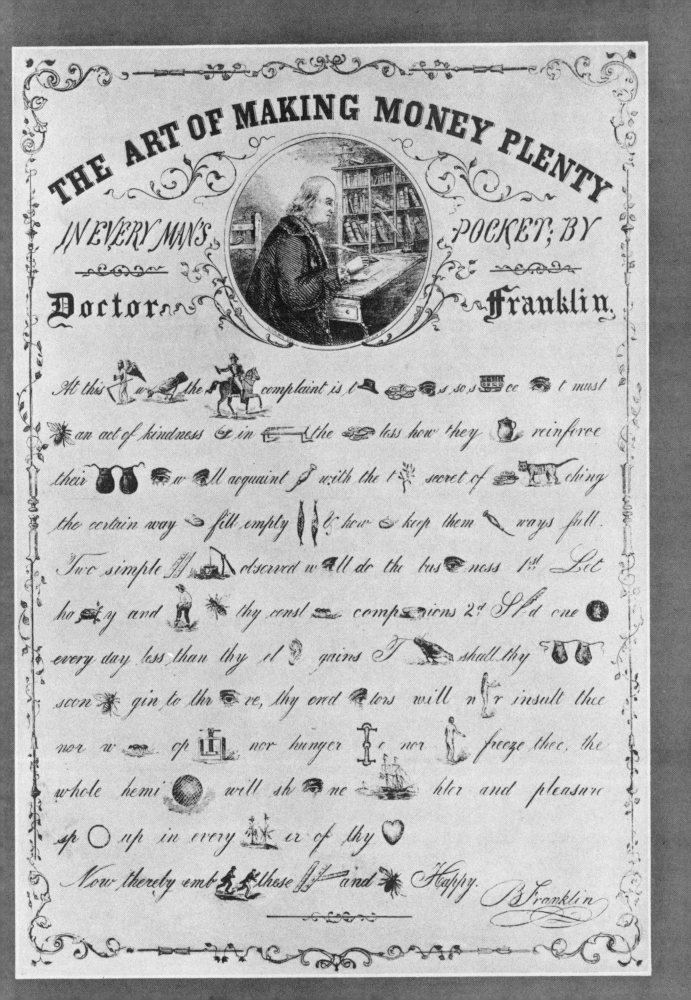

almanacs, Franklin's books contained information about the weather and tides, as well as recipes, poems, and calendars. They also included many wise and funny sayings which Franklin had made up himself. Ben Franklin was also interested in people. While he was in Philadelphia, he formed a club where he and his friends could gather to talk about important matters and enjoy each other's company. This later became the American Philosophical Society.*

As a man, Franklin's interest in reading and experimenting continued to grow. He taught himself to read books written in many languages, and he performed several important scientific experiments. In one of these, he proved that lightning is electricity. This made him famous all over Europe as well as in America.

A famous experiment. In 1752 Franklin proved that lightning is electricity.

The first lending library in the colonies was founded by Franklin at Philadelphia in 1731.

Franklin used his many interests and abilities to help other people. Through his club, he helped to improve the Philadelphia police department and to start the first fire department in the city. He also helped to establish the first hospital in Pennsylvania. Because he felt that learning was so important, he started the first lending library in the colonies and also founded a school that later became the University of Pennsylvania. To make life safer and more comfortable for other people, Franklin invented several useful articles. Among these were the lightning rod, the Franklin* stove, and bifocal* glasses. It is not surprising that Franklin became one of the best-loved citizens of Philadelphia.

Franklin's interests, however, spread beyond Philadelphia to America as a whole. When he was forty-two, he retired from

Franklin supervised the building of a frontier fort to protect the colonists against the Indians.

business and devoted most of his time to public service. He was deputy postmaster at Philadelphia, and later served as postmaster for all the colonies. He completely reformed the colonial postal system.

About this time, England and France were at war. The French were encouraging the Indians to attack the English colonists on the frontier. Franklin tried to persuade the different colonies to unite and work together to protect themselves against these attacks, but he was not successful. Then he helped to raise armies to defend the frontier colonists, and he supervised the building of a fort.

Franklin was also gravely concerned about the way the British government was treating the American colonies. Before the Revolutionary War* broke out, he was sent to England twice to help straighten out the difficulties between the colonies and the English government. At first, he did not feel that it was necessary for the colonies to become independent. He felt, however, that they should be treated fairly by the English government. Franklin did succeed in persuading the English to remove a heavy tax that had been established by the Stamp Act.* However, he finally realized that England never intended to treat the colonies as equals. When he returned to America in 1775, he entered wholeheartedly into his country's fight for freedom. He was one of the five men who prepared the Declaration of Independence.

Franklin was one of the signers of the Declaration of Independence, which he helped to prepare.

During and after the Revolutionary War, Benjamin Franklin served his country as minister* to France. His pleasant personality and his reputation as a scientist and scholar won him the love of many people in that country. He was able to persuade the French to provide the colonists with guns, ammunition, and food during their struggle for liberty.

Franklin returned to America in 1785, after serving his country as minister* to France.

Benjamin Franklin used his great talents to make life better for other people.

Though Franklin was a very old man when he returned to America from France, his days of service were not over. He worked with the men who wrote our country's Constitution. Later he became the president of the first antislavery* society in America. To the end of his eighty-four years, this great American kept his keen interest in the world around him. Throughout his lifetime he used his great talents to make life better for other people.

Thomas Jefferson helped to establish our democratic form of government. He was our third president.

Chapter 3
Thomas Jefferson
1743-1826

The United States is a democratic country. Our people have the right to choose the men and women who make our country's laws. A child from the poorest, humblest family in our land may someday become president.

Our government might have been different if Thomas Jefferson had not lived. At the close of the Revolutionary War,* some of

*See Glossary

our nation's leaders thought that men of wealth and education should control the government. They feared that the common people of America could not govern themselves wisely. It was partly because of Thomas Jefferson's faith in the common people that our form of democratic government was established.

It is surprising that Jefferson was on the side of the common people, for he came from a wealthy, landowning family. Mountains, streams, and deep forests surrounded his father's beautiful estate in Virginia. Here young Thomas rode horseback and paddled an Indian canoe. With his family and friends he enjoyed many good times.

Young Jefferson, however, was interested in more than pleasure. He wanted to learn about nature, the world around him, and the

On his father's beautiful estate, young Thomas Jefferson spent many happy boyhood years.

Preparing the Declaration of Independence. Jefferson was asked to write this important document.

ideas of other people. His father made careful plans for his education. Although Mr. Jefferson died when Thomas was only fourteen, the boy went on with his schooling just as his father had planned. He entered the College of William and Mary in Williamsburg, and graduated in two years. Next, he studied law. Even after he became a lawyer, he continued to read and study books in Greek, Latin, Italian, French, and English.

From the books he read and the people he met, Jefferson gained many new ideas about how people should be governed. He learned that great thinkers from other lands had said that all people, whether rich or poor, were born with certain rights. Jefferson felt that one of these was the right to help make their country's laws. The speeches of patriots, such as Patrick Henry,* helped him to see that the English government did not always give the colonists this right. Gradually, he came to believe that the colonists should break away from England and govern themselves. Jefferson wrote down many of his thoughts about government. His clear, forceful writings helped to influence the thinking of others.

Jefferson joined the colonial leaders who met in Philadelphia to decide whether the colonies should become independent. These leaders respected him greatly for his clear thinking and his writing ability. In 1776, he was asked to prepare a document explaining why the colonists wanted independence from England. This paper, the Declaration of Independence, is one of the most famous documents in American history.

Jefferson continued to work for freedom. After the colonies had won their independence from England, many Americans were not permitted to enjoy all their rights. In his own state, Virginia, many of the laws were not fair to everyone. People could not worship as they pleased. Many were not allowed to vote. As a member of Virginia's legislature, Jefferson helped to change these laws. Although Jefferson owned slaves himself, he worked to abolish slavery. He also worked to start a system of public education in Virginia. He was not successful in these efforts, but his writings on these subjects influenced many people.

During the years that followed the Revolutionary War, Jefferson did all he could to help the new American government become a true democracy. He served his country as a member of Congress, a minister* to France, and Secretary of State. He worked hard to inspire others with his belief that the common people were capable of taking part in the government. He also helped to form a political party to oppose those who thought a small ruling class should control the government.

Thomas Jefferson continued his work for democracy after he became president in 1801. Because he felt that the president should be treated as any other citizen, Jefferson wore plain clothes on the day of his inauguration,* and walked to the Capitol instead of driving in a carriage. During the eight years he was president, he lived and dressed very simply. Jefferson showed the people of the

Raising the flag in Louisiana. The Louisiana Purchase* was made while Jefferson was president.

A building designed by Jefferson for the University of Virginia. He helped to found this university.

United States that the president of a democracy really is the servant of the people.

While Jefferson was president, the United States doubled in size. In 1803, our government bought the vast territory of Louisiana from France. This extended the western boundary of the country to the Rocky Mountains.

Jefferson's last great gift to America was the University of Virginia. He worked hard to help establish this fine school, for he felt that though all people had the right to govern themselves, they could only do this well if they were educated.

The closing years of Jefferson's life were spent at his beautiful home, Monticello. He had designed this house himself, for in addition to being a great leader, he was also a fine architect. Here Jefferson had time to read, to experiment with scientific methods of farming, to visit with many friends, and to enjoy his grandchildren. He died on July 4, 1826, just fifty years after his famous Declaration of Independence had started America on the road to freedom.

Monticello. Jefferson was an architect as well as a great leader. He designed his own house.

President Abraham Lincoln. Without his leadership, our country might have been divided into two nations.

Chapter 4
Abraham Lincoln
1809-1865

   Abraham Lincoln was one of our greatest Americans. He had the wisdom to see what needed to be done in time of trouble. He also had the strength and courage to do what he saw was necessary, regardless of difficulty or danger. Without his wise, firm leadership at the time of the Civil War,* our country might have been divided into two separate nations.

*See Glossary

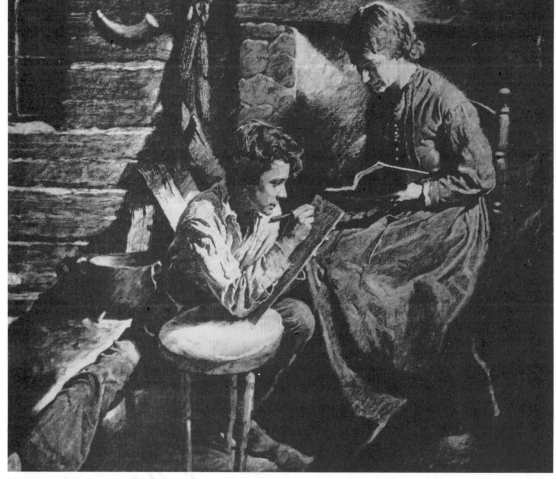

Young Abraham Lincoln was encouraged by his stepmother to read and study at home.

Lincoln's boyhood was different from that of most of our nation's leaders. He was born in a one-room log cabin in Kentucky. His father, a poor farmer, moved the family westward to the Indiana frontier when Abe was seven. Mr. Lincoln did not think education was important, and Abe had less than a year's schooling. Instead, he spent the days helping to clear the forest land and doing farm chores. When Abe was nine his mother died, and home became a dreary, cheerless place. Young Abe and his sister Sarah gave a warm welcome to the new wife their father later brought home. She was a kind, cheerful person. She encouraged Abe to read and study at home, even though his father thought this was a waste of time.

Young Abe's neighbors liked and respected him. He was much taller and stronger than most of his friends. No one in the county could beat him in a wrestling match or a footrace. He knew more jokes and funny stories than most people. At any gathering, he was usually the center of a crowd of laughing people. Abe had little schooling, but much of his time was spent reading books he borrowed from his neighbors. He was eager to learn.

Lincoln liked people, and he learned to understand them better through the many kinds of work he did. In Illinois, where he lived after he grew to manhood, Lincoln was a storekeeper, a postmaster, a captain of the militia, and a member of the state legislature. Later, he taught himself law and established a good law

Lincoln worked in a store, and he had several other jobs before he became a lawyer.

practice. During the years he practiced law, Lincoln also served one term in the United States House of Representatives.

Though he was a very successful lawyer, Abe Lincoln's chief interest was politics. He felt he could do more to solve his country's problems if he were active in the government.

Lincoln traveled across the prairies of Illinois, practicing law in the county courts.

Lincoln spoke in public on the problem of slavery. He believed that slavery was wrong.

One of the biggest problems in the United States at that time was slavery. In the early years of our country, many black slaves had been brought to the United States. Here they were sold just like horses, and made to work for their white owners. Slaves were used mainly in the southern states, for many workers were needed on the huge cotton plantations in this farming region. In the North, where many farms were small and there were many factories, slave labor was not as useful. The northern states soon passed laws forbidding slavery in their part of the country. In Lincoln's time the big question was whether or not slavery should be permitted in the new states which were then joining the Union.*

People in the South thought it should be allowed. People in the North did not think so. The two sections of the country quarreled bitterly over this question.

Lincoln felt that slavery was wrong and should not be allowed in the new states. He wanted to do something about this. In 1854 and again in 1858, he decided to run for the United States Senate. In his political campaigns for this position, he made many speeches explaining his thoughts about slavery. He gave some of his most famous speeches in a series of debates* with Stephen A. Douglas, the man who was running against him for the office of senator. Although Lincoln did not win either election, his speeches made

Lincoln became president in 1861. He promised to preserve, protect, and defend the Union.

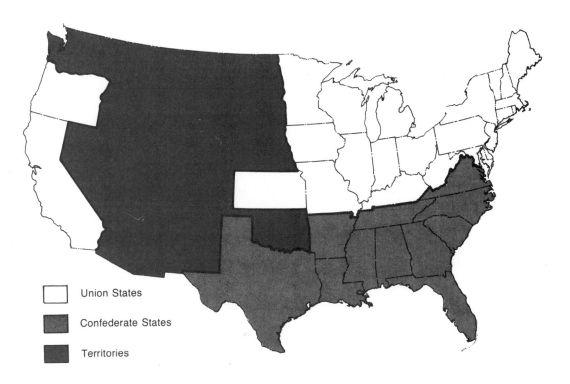

A divided country. Lincoln fought the Civil War to bring our country back together.

Union States

Confederate States

Territories

him well known all over the country. Two years later, in 1860, he was elected president of the United States.

The people of the southern states were unhappy about Lincoln's election. They knew he would try to keep slavery out of the new states. They also feared that under his leadership the government would try to forbid slavery in the South. To keep this from happening, many of the southern states withdrew from the Union.

Lincoln understood how the southern people felt. In the speech he made when he became president, he promised not to interfere with slavery in the southern states. He asked that Northerners and Southerners work together to keep the country united. "We are not enemies but friends," he said. "We must not be enemies."

In spite of his words, the southern states that had left the Union refused to return. They formed a separate country, the Confederate States of America. A weaker leader might have let them stay out. Lincoln, however, did not permit this. He knew that if these states left the Union, other states would also feel they could become independent whenever they wanted to. This would break our strong, united country into several small, weak nations.

Lincoln did not want to fight a war to preserve the Union. However, once the Civil War began, he led the northern states firmly and courageously to victory. During this terrible struggle, he issued an order called the Emancipation Proclamation,* which led to freedom for the slaves. Never again would the question of slavery divide the country. At last, the words "all men are created equal" were starting to become a reality.

After the surrender of the main Confederate forces in 1865, Lincoln started the great task of restoring his war-torn country. He did not have time to complete his work, however. On the evening of April 14, he attended a play with his wife and some

Lincoln reading the Emancipation Proclamation.* This document led to the end of slavery.

Lincoln's statue in Washington, D.C., reminds us that this great leader kept our country united.

friends. Suddenly, a shot rang through the theater. The startled audience saw an actor named John Wilkes Booth leap from the President's box, and leave the building. For a moment, no one understood what had happened. Then the terrible news swept through the room. Lincoln had been shot.

Although Lincoln died more than one hundred years ago, his leadership and courage are still an example to Americans everywhere.

Harriet Beecher Stowe was a writer. Her book *Uncle Tom's Cabin* helped cause the Civil War.

Chapter 5
Harriet Beecher Stowe
1811-1896

On the day after Thanksgiving, 1862, a small, curly-haired woman visited President Lincoln in the White House in Washington, D.C. Her name was Harriet Beecher Stowe and she had come to ask an important question. Did President Lincoln plan to free *all* the slaves in the United States?

When Harriet Beecher Stowe asked this question, a terrible struggle called the Civil War was going on in our country. The southern states, which permitted slavery, had broken away from the northern states, where slavery was not allowed. But the North refused to let the South go without a fight.

The powerful country of Britain was trying to decide whose side to be on in the Civil War. Most people in Britain thought slavery was wrong. However, the British were not sure that Lincoln would free the slaves in the South, even if the North won the war. Besides, Britain needed cotton that was raised on plantations* in the South for its cloth mills. So Britain was thinking about siding with the South.

*See Glossary

Cotton from southern plantations was used in British cloth mills. The British considered siding with the South in the Civil War even though they hated slavery.

After Harriet Beecher Stowe's visit with President Lincoln, she wrote a letter to twenty-two of the most important women in Britain. Mrs. Stowe told these women that President Lincoln *did* plan to free the slaves in the South if the North won the war. But if the South won, they would remain in slavery. Mrs. Stowe's letter was printed in a well-known magazine. It helped the British leaders make up their minds not to side with the South. This helped the North to win the Civil War.

A Civil War battle. Mrs. Stowe helped convince the British not to side with the South.

Why did the British listen to Harriet Beecher Stowe? Her childhood gives us part of the answer. Harriet was born in a part of our country called New England.* Her father was a well-known preacher named Lyman Beecher. He helped Harriet and her brothers and sisters to think seriously about right and wrong, and to work hard for what they thought was right.

Harriet began to read the books in her father's library when she was just six years old. When she was twelve, she wrote a school paper that was so good the principal read it out loud at graduation. Harriet attended a high school that had been started by her older sister Catherine. In Harriet's time, girls were expected to learn to be good homemakers, not to study subjects like science and history. Catherine did not agree with this idea. Her school taught girls both kinds of knowledge. After Harriet finished this school she became one of its teachers.

When Harriet was still a young woman, the Beecher family moved south to the city of Cincinnati, Ohio. Lyman became the president of a seminary* there, and Catherine started a girls' school. Harriet taught in her sister's school and wrote stories and articles for magazines in her spare time. While she was in Cincinnati, Harriet met and married Professor Calvin Stowe, and had a big family. She stopped teaching, but she continued to write.

Cincinnati was very different from New England. This city was just across a river from the southern state of Kentucky. For the first time, Harriet saw slaves being bought and sold. She saw families separated as the father was sold to one person and the mother to another.

Until that time, Harriet had not thought much about whether slavery was right or wrong. Neither had many other Americans.

Slaves were property. Mrs. Stowe saw slaves being bought and sold after she moved south.

A small group of people called Abolitionists thought slavery should be ended right away, even if this caused problems for both the slaves and their owners. Most people thought the Abolitionists were troublemakers. Harriet did not agree with the Abolitionists, either. But she came to feel that some orderly way should be found to end slavery.

In 1850, Harriet and her husband and children moved back to New England. About this time, something happened that made Harriet and many other people in the North very angry. The United States government passed a law that slaves who escaped to the North had to be returned to their owners. Everyone had to help catch them and send them back, even people who believed slavery was wrong.

Harriet felt the time had come when she must do something that would help bring slavery to an end. She decided to write a magazine story that would make people understand the terrible things slavery did to people's lives. It would be a continuing story that would be published one chapter at a time.

Runaway slaves had to be returned to their owners. This made Harriet Beecher Stowe so angry that she wrote a story showing how slavery hurt people's lives.

UNCLE TOM'S CABIN;

OR,

LIFE AMONG THE LOWLY.

BY

HARRIET BEECHER STOWE.

VOL. I.

BOSTON:
JOHN P. JEWETT & COMPANY.
CLEVELAND, OHIO:
JEWETT, PROCTOR & WORTHINGTON.
1852.

The characters in Harriet's story were so real that thousands of people became interested in them. Her readers would wait impatiently for the magazine to come out each week to find out what happened next. When the story was finished, it was published as a book called *Uncle Tom's Cabin.* This quickly became one of the best-selling books in the world.

Uncle Tom's Cabin was a very important book. It made people throughout the North agree for the first time that slavery had to be ended. But in the South, *Uncle Tom's Cabin* only made people angry. Southerners felt the book gave a false picture of slavery. The bad feelings between the two sides helped to bring on the Civil War.

Uncle Tom's Cabin made Harriet Beecher Stowe one of the best-known women of her time. She was invited to Britain to make speeches against slavery. Huge crowds greeted her everywhere she went, and she made friends with many important people. This is why the British were willing to listen when she said that they should not side with the South in the Civil War.

Harriet Beecher Stowe lived for many years after the Civil War. When the war was over, she encouraged people in the North and South to live together as friends. She spent her winters in Florida, and wrote a book that helped other people in the North decide to spend winters there, too. She also wrote several books about life in New England. But Harriet Beecher Stowe is remembered best for *Uncle Tom's Cabin,* the book that helped bring about the war that ended slavery in the United States.

Uncle Tom's Cabin became one of the most popular books in the world. It convinced people in the North that slavery had to be ended.

Joseph was a chief of the Nez Percé Indians. He tried to help Americans realize that all people are brothers and everyone in our country should have equal rights.

Chapter 6
Chief Joseph
1840(?)-1904

The Nez Percé Indians loved the quiet, peaceful Wallowa Valley. It was one of the most beautiful places in Oregon. The Nez Percés lived in small villages along several rivers in the valley. There they were free to live as they had always lived. They roamed the forests and plains, fishing, hunting, and raising horses for a living. The Nez Percés were a gentle people, and the Wallowa Valley was a gentle place.

The Nez Percés loved Joseph, their chief, as much as they loved their home. Joseph was a strong but kindly man. He stood six feet tall and was handsome and very able. Joseph was a skilled warrior, but he did not like war. His people admired his courage and strength. They also admired his love of peace.

In 1877 trouble came to Chief Joseph. For many years white settlers had been moving closer and closer to the valley. They,

White settlers traveling to Oregon. During the 1800's many settlers moved westward.

too, thought it was a beautiful place, and they wanted it for themselves. Soldiers were sent by the United States government to move the Nez Percés to a reservation* many miles away.

The Nez Percés did not want to go to the reservation. It was not as beautiful as the Wallowa Valley, and they would have less freedom there. Many Nez Percé braves wanted to fight the soldiers who had come to move them from their homes. Joseph did not want to move either. He loved his freedom also, but he knew that many of his people would die if war started. The United States government had more soldiers than the Nez Percés. To avoid war, Joseph sadly agreed to take his people to the reservation.

Before Joseph could move his people, a handful of braves killed several white settlers. They did this against Joseph's wishes. Their actions caused him much sadness. "I would have given my own life if I could have undone the killing of white men by my people," Joseph said.

It was too late. General Oliver Howard saw the killing as an act of war. He quickly sent soldiers to attack the Nez Percés in the Wallowa Valley. Now Joseph had no choice but to fight. He had to protect his people. Joseph was a peaceful man, but he was also a great military leader. The soldiers had better guns than the Nez Percés, but Joseph knew the Wallowa Valley. After all, his people had lived there for many years. Under Joseph's leadership, sixty Nez Percé warriors defeated General Howard's army. Some of General Howard's soldiers were wounded and captured, but they were not harmed after the battle. "We do not believe in scalping," Joseph said, "nor in killing wounded men."

Joseph knew that more soldiers would soon come to the valley. He also realized that his people would not go willingly to the reservation. Joseph decided to lead the Nez Percés east to Montana. From there, they would go to Canada, where they could live in freedom.

50

*See Glossary

Carrying what little they had, the Nez Percés began their long journey. Some rode horses and others walked. In Montana, Joseph led his band of seven hundred into the mountains. He hoped that here he could escape from the white soldiers.

Traveling through the mountains was very hard. There was little food and the weather was cold. The Indians had no blankets

Traveling through the mountains. Joseph hoped to escape from the white soldiers by traveling through the mountains to Canada. The weather in the mountains was very cold.

to protect them from the biting, cold wind. More than half of Joseph's followers were women and children. Some of the children froze to death. Still the Nez Percés followed Joseph through the mountains. They believed in him and they took comfort in his strength. They knew Chief Joseph was trying to lead them to freedom.

In eleven weeks Joseph and his people covered more than 1,000 miles of rough country. There were soldiers to fight at every turn. By now, Joseph's braves were tired and hungry. Yet, they followed him into battle thirteen times against the soldiers. They won nearly every battle. Joseph's skill and cleverness surprised the soldiers. Time after time, he escaped their rifle bullets.

The hard journey weakened the Indians. The terrible cold weather had gotten worse and the Indians were starving and dying. Canada was only forty miles away. But could the children and old people in Joseph's group go any farther?

Fighting near the Big Hole River in Montana. The Indians and soldiers fought many times.

Joseph surrendered because his people were too tired and hungry to go any farther.

In September of 1877, Chief Joseph made the hardest decision of his life. He went to General Howard's camp and surrendered. "I am tired of fighting," said Joseph. "Our chiefs are killed . . . It is cold, and we have no blankets. The little children are freezing to death. My people, some of them, have run away to the hills, and have no blankets, no food . . . I want to have time to look for my children, and see how many of them I can find. . ."

Chief Joseph was only thirty-seven when he gave up his freedom to General Howard's soldiers. He could have left the weak and sick people in his group behind and gone on to Canada. But instead, he surrendered and went with them to a reservation.

In 1879, Joseph went to Washington, D.C., to ask the government leaders to let his people go home. He spoke from his heart. "...All men were made by the same Great Spirit Chief. They are all brothers. The earth is the mother of all people, and all people should have equal rights upon it." Today, thoughtful people agree that the words of this great American describe the only way that people can live together in peace.

A group of Nez Percé Indians on a reservation. Chief Joseph went to Washington, D. C., to ask the government to let his people go back to their home.

Susan B. Anthony helped women gain the right to vote.

Chapter 7

Susan B. Anthony
1820-1906

Little Susan Anthony looked around her as she walked through her father's cotton mill in Battenville, New York. One of the machines had stopped working. The man in charge of the workers didn't know what was wrong with it. "Sally Ann," he called to a woman worker. "Come fix this machine."

Susan Anthony watched as Sally Ann quickly got the machine running. This woman knew much more about weaving than the man. Susan wondered why she wasn't in charge. Her father explained that people would not accept a woman overseer* at the mill. They weren't used to having women in positions like that.

In the 1820's, when Susan was a girl, women had very few rights. Most kinds of jobs were closed to women. A woman received less pay for any job than a man who did the same kind of work. There were laws that said a married woman could not own property. Everything she owned belonged to her husband. Her husband could take away any money she earned. She did not even have a right to her children. Her husband could take them away if he wished.

There was no way for women to improve their situation. It was against the law for them to vote. They were not even permitted to speak in most public meetings. They had very little opportunity for education. Most people thought that girls needed only to know how to care for a home.

Susan Anthony was more fortunate than most girls. Her family were Quakers,* who believed that women were equal with men before God. At Quaker meetings, women were encouraged to speak if they had something helpful to say. In Quaker families, girls as well as boys were educated. Susan's father set aside a special room in their house for a school. When Susan finished this school, she became a teacher for a while. Then she went away to a boarding school in Philadelphia for more education.

Susan's family was interested in other problems besides equal rights for women. Millions of black Americans were slaves who could be bought and sold. Many American families were being hurt because a parent drank too much alcohol.* Susan and her family felt that something should be done about all of these problems.

*See Glossary

When Susan was eighteen, her father's business failed and she had to stop school. To help her father pay his debts, she became a teacher, first in the town of New Rochelle, then in a town called Canajoharie in New York State. In her spare time, she worked with temperance* groups, which encouraged people not to drink alcohol.

Girls in Susan B. Anthony's time did not usually have much opportunity for education.

When Susan was in her late twenties, she stopped teaching. She continued to work with temperance groups. She also attended meetings of people who wanted to end slavery. Some of the women she met at these meetings were also working on women's rights.

In 1848, Susan tried to speak at a large temperance meeting in Albany, New York. The men in charge told her that "the sisters had not been invited here to speak, but to listen and to learn." Susan and several other women left the meeting and organized a new group called the Woman's State Temperance Society of New York.

As time went on, Susan became more and more interested in women's rights. In 1854, she decided to try to help change the law that prevented women in the state of New York from owning property. Susan traveled from town to town with a petition. This was a paper that asked the state lawmakers to change the law. It was winter, and the weather was snowy. Susan went from door to door in the cold. She asked women to sign her petition. Some people slammed the door in her face. However, many thousands of people signed the petition. Even so, the lawmakers refused to change the law.

This defeat did not discourage Susan. She went from town to town arranging meetings where people could listen to speeches about women's rights. She also organized conventions. These were large meetings where women from different towns could gather to discuss their needs and problems. Finally, in 1860, the lawmakers of New York passed a new law that gave women the right to own property and to keep their earnings when they worked outside the home.

Susan B. Anthony continued to care about other things besides women's rights. After the Civil War,* she helped to form the American Equal Rights Association. This group worked to help the newly-freed blacks win their rights. She also started a magazine called *The Revolution.* It discussed the problems of factory workers and blacks as well as women.

Susan's main interest, however was women's rights. As time went on, she came to feel the most important thing women needed was the right to vote. This right is known as woman suffrage. In 1869, Susan and her friend Elizabeth Cady Stanton formed the National Woman Suffrage Association to work for the right to vote.

Susan B. Anthony spoke about woman suffrage in hundreds of towns and cities.

Insulting cartoons made fun of women who were working for women's rights.

Most people in the 1800's thought that woman suffrage was a foolish idea. Some got very angry about it. They made sarcastic jokes about people who were working for women's right to vote. Susan's magazine, *The Revolution,* bravely published articles about this unpopular subject.

Susan worked hard to make *The Revolution* a success. She edited*
articles, took the paper to the printer, and sold advertising. People in many parts of the country became interested in *The Revolution*. However, Susan was not able to sell enough copies of the paper to pay for publishing it. Finally, the magazine was $10,000 in debt, and she had to give it up.

Susan wanted to pay the paper's debt. To earn money, she went all over the United States making paid speeches about woman suffrage. By the time the debt was paid, thousands of people had heard Susan B. Anthony speak.

Susan felt that talking about woman suffrage was not enough. In November, 1872, she entered the building in her hometown where people were voting for president. The man in charge told

Susan B. Anthony voted for president in 1872. She was arrested for breaking the law.

her it was against the laws of New York for her to vote. She voted anyway. By the end of the day, fifteen other women in the community had followed her example.

Susan B. Anthony was arrested and brought to trial for breaking the law. Newspapers all over the country carried news about the trial. Some of them made fun of her. Others printed thoughtful articles about what she was trying to do.

Susan B. Anthony worked for women's rights until she was a very old woman.

Women marched through the streets demanding the vote. This right was granted in 1920.

As the years passed, people all over the world began to pay attention to Susan B. Anthony. In 1888, women from England, France, Norway, Denmark, Finland, India, and Canada came to a meeting in Washington, D.C., which she helped to organize. In 1904, Susan Anthony traveled to Germany, where she helped form the International Woman Suffrage Alliance. By 1919, women in fifteen countries outside the United States had gained the right to vote.

In 1920, women in the United States finally gained the right to vote. Susan B. Anthony was not alive to see her dream come true. But Americans today can thank this brave woman for the part she played in helping our country.

Franklin Roosevelt was our president during the Great Depression and World War II.

Chapter 8
Franklin and Eleanor Roosevelt
Franklin 1882-1945   Eleanor 1884-1962

In 1932, many Americans had to wait in long lines for free food. They would much rather have worked to earn money to buy food. But they could not find jobs. The United States was in a depression.* People felt hopeless and afraid. Hard times like this had happened before. But they had always ended after a short while. This depression showed no signs of ending. It went on so long that we call it the Great Depression.

*See Glossary

On a chilly day in March, 1933, a new president took office who promised to try to get people back to work. His name was Franklin Delano Roosevelt. A crowd of one hundred thousand people stood outside the White House to hear Roosevelt's inaugural* speech. Millions more listened to his words on radio. "The only thing we have to fear is fear itself," Roosevelt told his listeners. Under his leadership, the government of the United States would not simply wait for things to get better. It would take action.

To many of the people listening, this confident, handsome man seemed to have been born to be president. His family was one of the oldest and best known in the United States. One of his relatives, Theodore Roosevelt, had been our twenty-sixth president.

People standing in line for government jobs. Roosevelt believed the government should use its power to help people with their problems. Not everyone agreed with this idea.

Franklin spent most of his childhood on his father's beautiful estate at Hyde Park, New York. He was an only child, and his parents showered him with love and attention. He had few playmates, but he enjoyed swimming, riding horseback, and skating. In summer, Franklin's family often took him on trips to Europe. When he was fourteen, he was sent to boarding school at Groton, Massachusetts. Later, he attended Harvard University. After he graduated in 1904, Roosevelt studied law at Columbia University in New York.

Franklin Roosevelt was an only child. His parents showered him with love and attention.

Eleanor Roosevelt married Franklin in 1905. Her childhood was not as happy as Franklin's.

When Franklin was twenty three, he married Theodore Roosevelt's niece, Eleanor Roosevelt. Like Franklin, Eleanor had grown up in a wealthy home. But her family life had not been happy. Her father had left the home when she was very little. Since she was not beautiful like her mother and aunts, she had never felt important. However, Eleanor Roosevelt was honest, caring, and intelligent.

During their first years of marriage, Franklin worked as a lawyer and Eleanor spent her time raising a family. In 1910, Franklin

Campaigning for the office of vice-president in 1920. Roosevelt went into politics in 1910. First he was elected to the lawmaking body of New York. Then he was nominated for vice-president.

decided that politics* would be more interesting and exciting. His first goal was to be elected to the New York State Senate.* In a bright-red car he drove to almost every crossroad and village in his political* district. He shook hands, made speeches, and won friends. These friends voted for him. He became the first Democrat* to be elected state senator by the people in his district in thirty-two years.

In 1913, Franklin Roosevelt was appointed Assistant Secretary of the Navy. Roosevelt had always loved the sea. When the United States entered World War I* in 1917, he worked hard to help make the Navy a strong fighting force. After the war, he was nominated for the office of vice-president of the United States. Even though he did not win this election, his name was becoming well known to the American people.

Eleanor was not so well known. She had been busy taking care of her home and family. Until World War I, she did not pay much attention to what was going on in the world. Then one day she visited a hospital for servicemen whose minds had been hurt by

Eleanor Roosevelt with four of her children. Franklin and Eleanor had six children.

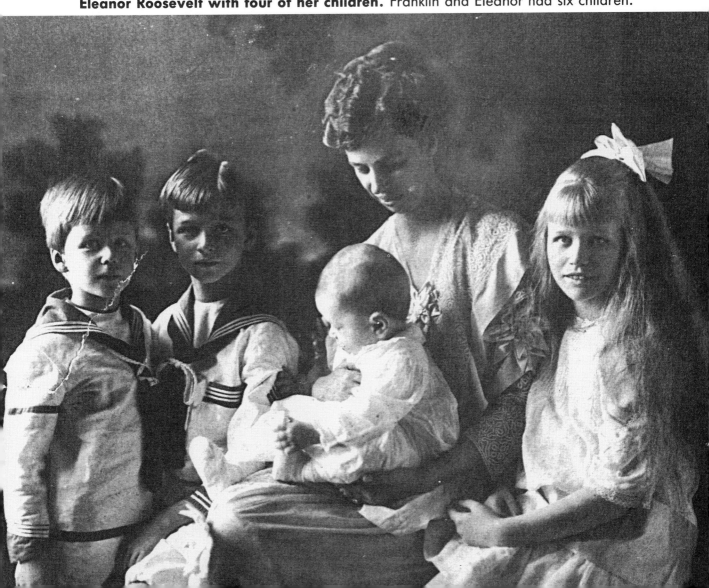

their war experiences. She was shocked at how poorly these sick people were treated. Eleanor worked to improve the hospital. This experience helped her realize there were problems in the world she could help to solve.

In August, 1921, the lives of Eleanor and Franklin Roosevelt were greatly changed. Franklin became ill with a terrible disease called polio. He got well again, but he could no longer walk. The muscles in his legs were paralyzed.* Both Franklin and Eleanor were determined not to let the illness defeat him. During years of pain and discouragement they never lost hope. Franklin learned to walk with crutches, then with a cane, and finally with heavy, steel braces.

Roosevelt's illness seemed to give him even greater courage and strength. It also made him a more patient and sympathetic per-

Roosevelt became governor of New York for the second time, on January 1, 1931.

son. With Eleanor's encouragement, he returned to politics. In a short time he won the confidence of the whole nation. In 1928 he was elected governor of New York State. Soon afterwards, the Great Depression started. Knowing about the hopelessness and anger people felt, Roosevelt decided to run for president.

Franklin Delano Roosevelt was elected president for four terms. During the years he was president, our country changed in very important ways. Until this time, most Americans felt that government should interfere in business as little as possible. People were expected to take care of their own problems. If they needed help, it came mainly from churches and other private groups.

Roosevelt believed that the United States government should use its power to help people. He started a plan called the "New Deal." Under the New Deal, the government spent billions of dollars in tax money to build roads, dams, and public buildings. Millions of unemployed people were put to work on these government projects. The government loaned money to banks and businesses that were in danger of failing. It provided money for people who were in danger of losing their homes and farms because they could not make payments on them. Government money was also given to old people, to blind people, and to needy mothers and children.

Eleanor worked hard to help her husband after he became president. In a way, she became his legs. She went across our country, talking to people. When she got back to the White House, she would tell Franklin what people thought and said.

Eleanor helped people in her own way, also. She spoke out when people were treated unfairly because of their race. She called meetings with newspaper reporters at the White House. A president's wife had never done this before. Eleanor talked to the

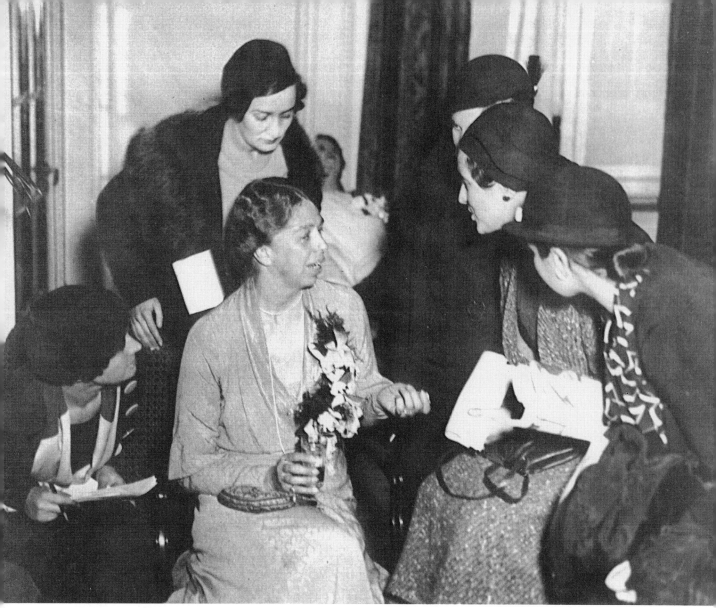

Eleanor talked to people in many parts of the United States. She told Franklin what they thought and said. She held meetings with newspaper reporters.

newspaper people about things that could make people's lives better.

Soon after Roosevelt had been elected president for the third time, the United States entered World War II.* Roosevelt worked with the leaders of Britain and other friendly countries to win the war. Eleanor traveled all over the world, visiting American service men and women in hospitals and military camps.

Franklin Delano Roosevelt died in 1945, a year after he had been elected president for the fourth time. By that time, millions of people had come to love and trust him. They agreed with his idea that the government should try to help solve people's problems. There were others who felt this idea was wrong. Both sides, however,

Franklin Roosevelt led our nation through World War II.

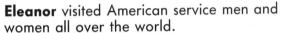

Eleanor visited American service men and women all over the world.

agreed that the United States had been greatly changed by Roosevelt's bold leadership.

Eleanor thought her work was done when Franklin died. This was not so. In 1945, President Truman asked her to be our country's representative to a new peace-keeping group called the United

73

Nations.* Her patience and intelligence helped this organization through its first difficult years. Under her leadership, the United Nations accepted an important document called the Universal Declaration of Human Rights.* As people read this document, they realized that Eleanor Roosevelt was not only a great American, but she had also become a great citizen of the world.

Eleanor speaking at the United Nations. After Franklin's death in 1945, Eleanor became our country's representative to this peace-keeping organization.

Martin Luther King, Jr., made the United States begin to live up to its promise of being a country in which all people are created equal.

Chapter 9
Martin Luther King, Jr., and Coretta Scott King
Martin 1929-1968   Coretta 1927-

August 28, 1963, was a bright clear day in Washington, D.C. Even though the sun was hot, 250,000 people had gathered in our country's capital. They had come from all over America. Some had come in old cars and crowded buses. Others had come by airplane or train. Many had walked to Washington,D.C., from faraway places. They had come to demand that the United States be the kind of country it said it was...a country in which all people are equal.

In 1963, Martin Luther King Jr., spoke to a crowd of 250,000 people in Washington, D.C. They had come to demand that blacks be given their rights as American citizens.

By noon the great crowd stretched from the Lincoln Memorial to the Washington Monument. Everywhere there were people, almost as far as you could see. They were all looking up at a young black minister* named Martin Luther King, Jr. As he stood to speak, thundering waves of applause rose from the crowd. Then, as if by magic, the huge crowd began to chant his name.

*See Glossary

"I have a dream," he said, "that one day . . .the sons of former slaves and the sons of former slaveowners will be able to sit down together at the table of brotherhood."

The crowd quieted, and Martin Luther King, Jr., began to speak. He told the world why this great crowd had assembled. He told the people gathered here to keep on with their task of making our nation live up to its promises. And then he shared a dream . . . a dream that the United States would one day be a nation in which all people were treated fairly.

Whites and blacks were separated by law in the South. This is called segregation.

The United States was not this kind of nation when Martin Luther King, Jr., was a boy. In the South, where Martin was born, there were laws that kept blacks from enjoying many freedoms. Blacks were not allowed to sit with whites in eating places or on buses. They were not allowed in many hotels and public places, such as parks and swimming pools. Black children were not allowed to attend the same schools as white children. Separating people by law this way is called segregation.

In the North, blacks were not separated from whites by law. But because of prejudice* they were still not treated fairly. Black people could not buy houses or rent apartments in most white neighborhoods. They were not hired for good jobs by businesses. Unfair treatment like this is called discrimination.

Segregation and discrimination made the lives of black Americans very difficult. The schools most of them attended were not very good. The jobs that were open to them usually did not pay well. Being kept out of nice places made it difficult for many of them to feel they were as good as other people.

Martin Luther King, Jr., was more fortunate than many blacks. His father was a respected minister in Atlanta, Georgia. His mother was a teacher. They lived in a nice house. As a boy, Martin loved to listen to this father's sermons. From the age of six, he was very active in his father's church. When he sang hymns, Martin often moved people to tears. He was bright and kind. People loved to be around him.

Some of Martin's playmates were white children who lived near the Kings' house. One day Martin rushed home in tears. The parents of his white friends told him he could no longer play with their children. The only reason was the color of his skin. This was one of Martin's first experiences with prejudice. It hurt him so deeply that he never forgot it. Such early experiences shaped Martin's plans. He wanted to help improve life for blacks in America. He wanted to fight for freedom and equal rights for all Americans.

While attending Morehouse College in Atlanta, Martin decided to become a minister. At eighteen, he became assistant minister of the Ebenezer Baptist Church. This was his father's church. Martin Luther King, Jr., was a powerful speaker. He made people think.

Whenever he spoke, people wanted to shout with enthusiasm for what he was saying.

Martin Luther King, Jr., went on for more education after he finished Morehouse College. While he was attending Boston University, he met a music student named Coretta Scott. A short while later, Martin asked Coretta to marry him.

At first, Coretta was not sure she wanted to marry Martin. Coretta's family had worked hard to give her the opportunity for an education. The Scotts lived in Perry County, Alabama. There was a high school for white children ten miles from their house. The nearest high school for blacks was twenty miles away. Mrs. Scott arranged for Coretta and her sister to stay with a family and attend a private school in the city of Marion.

In Coretta's senior year, she won a scholarship to Antioch College in Yellow Springs, Ohio. Coretta studied to be a music teacher in college. She needed to do practice teaching. But the Yellow Springs school board would not let her teach in the public schools. Hurt and angry she agreed to do her practice teaching in the private school run by the college. She also joined several groups at the school that were working to change the way black people were treated.

Coretta's teachers at Antioch thought her voice was so beautiful she should go on for more training. She received a grant* to study voice at the Boston Conservatory of Music. Coretta was ambitious. She wanted to see if she could become a famous singer. But she also loved Martin Luther King, Jr. She shared his dream of helping to make the United States live up to its promise of being a place where everyone was equal. In 1953, Coretta and Martin were married.

Dinner in the King home. In 1953, Martin Luther King, Jr., married Coretta Scott. Coretta shared Martin's dream of making the United States a country where everyone was treated fairly. To make this dream come true, the Kings followed the teachings of a great leader named Mahatma Gandhi who had helped the country of India peacefully win its independence from Britain. Gandhi's picture is shown on the wall in this photograph.

Speaking to reporters in Montgomery. Martin Luther King, Jr., and Coretta moved to Montgomery, Alabama in 1954. They helped to organize a bus boycott* in this city.

In 1954, a church in Montgomery, Alabama asked Martin Luther King, Jr., to be its minister. Like other cities in the South, Montgomery was segregated. Blacks were treated with disrespect here. Their treatment was especially bad on city buses.

On December 1, 1955, a black woman named Mrs. Rosa Parks was arrested by the Montgomery police. She had boarded a bus and sat in the section where blacks were supposed to sit. Soon the bus became crowded. All the seats for white people were filled. The bus driver told Rosa Parks to get up and give her seat to a white person. Rosa's feet hurt and she was tired. Besides, she was in the section of the bus reserved for blacks. So she refused to move and was arrested.

When Dr. King heard about Rosa Parks' arrest, he met with the other black leaders in Montgomery. They decided to demonstrate,* or show the white leaders of Montgomery that blacks wanted to be treated with respect on buses. They would do this by refusing to ride the bus. The blacks in Montgomery chose Martin Luther King, Jr., to be the leader of this bus boycott.* He and Coretta worked day and night, arranging rides and doing other jobs to organize the boycott, which went on for a year. This seriously hurt the bus company's business. In the end the United States government said that bus companies everywhere had to treat all their riders the same!

This was the beginning of a great freedom movement in the United States. Over the next few years, Dr. King led demonstrations and

Marching to Montgomery. Coretta and Martin Luther King, Jr., led many demonstrations.*

Blacks peacefully broke the unfair law that kept them from sitting at lunch counters.

gave speeches in cities throughout our country. At first he worked only for blacks. As time went on, he worked for poor white people and Spanish-speaking people also. With Coretta's help, he inspired thousands of people to stand up against injustice.

Martin Luther King, Jr., insisted that his followers work for change peacefully. He told them they should simply stop obeying unfair laws. If they were arrested for breaking these laws, he told them not to fight back. When enough peaceful people had been arrested, he knew the leaders would have to change unfair laws.

Dr. King was arrested many times. He spent many long, lonely nights in jail for his beliefs. This was very hard for Coretta. Yet, she helped him in every way. She sang in concerts to raise money for his work. She spoke to groups of people when Dr. King could not do so.

Martin and Coretta's beliefs led them into danger. Their home was bombed. Dr. King led marches in cities where hatred of blacks was strong. He was kicked and beaten. Vicious dogs were turned loose on his followers. But Dr. King refused to fight violence* with violence. He knew the truth was more powerful than guns or clubs.

Martin Luther King, Jr., went to jail many times for peacefully breaking unfair laws.

Signing the Civil Rights Act of 1964. This act made discrimination unlawful.

Martin Luther King, Jr.'s plan for changing laws was successful. In 1964, President Johnson signed the Civil Rights Act. This was a law that gave all people in the United States the right to go to public places like parks, swimming pools, and hotels. It forbade employers to close jobs to people for reasons such as race. It also required people in charge of elections to treat everyone who came to vote in the same way.

People throughout the world came to admire Martin Luther King for his peaceful ways of changing unjust laws. In 1964, he received the Nobel Peace Prize* in Norway. This prize included both money and a medal. Dr. King gave the money to groups that were working to help change unfair laws. He said the prize was not just for him, but for "all men who love peace and brotherhood."

With King Olav of Norway. Martin Luther King, Jr., received the Nobel Peace Prize* in Norway.

Martin Luther King, Jr., was hated as much as he was admired. He was hated by people who did not want to see the changes he was helping to make. On April 4, 1968, one of these people murdered him as he stood on a motel balcony in Memphis, Tennessee.

Dr. King's life was cut short, but the idea he lived for lives on. Today, Coretta Scott King carries on the work she and her husband began together. Martin Luther and Coretta King gave the world the gift of hope...hope that people of every color will one day live together in freedom and dignity.

Coretta Scott King continued to work for freedom after her husband was murdered.

Horace Mann helped the people of the United States see the need for good public schools.

Chapter 10
Horace Mann
1796-1859

A cold draft blew through the dreary little schoolhouse in Franklin, Massachusetts. The children sitting on the rickety wooden benches shivered, and huddled closer together. The books they were studying were uninteresting and hard to understand.

No maps or charts hung on the drab schoolroom walls. The teacher was untrained and poorly paid.

Young Horace Mann did not mind the cold, ugly room or the untrained teacher. He was thankful to be able to attend school at all. Classes were held for only a few weeks each summer and a few more weeks each winter. During the summer, he had to help with the work on his father's small, sandy farm. That left him only the short winter session to attend school. If only people would vote to spend enough money to keep the public school open

A country school. As a boy, Horace Mann was able to attend school for only a few weeks each year.

for a longer time! Or, better yet, if only his father had enough money to send him to a good private school!

Horace Mann was more fortunate than most children from poor families at this time. Even though he had little schooling as a child, he was able to make up for it later. When he was twenty, he met a good teacher from a private high school. Horace studied hard with this teacher for six months. At the end of that time, he had learned so much that he was admitted to Brown University. He graduated from Brown with honors and entered law school.

Though Horace Mann became a very successful lawyer, his chief interest was in education. He could not forget the dreary, little school he had attended as a boy. When he was elected to the Massachusetts State Legislature he began working to improve public education in his state. In 1837, he helped to pass a law which established a state board of education for Massachusetts.

Horace Mann felt that he could do even more to help improve the schools in Massachusetts. He gave up his law practice and his position in the Senate to become the secretary of the new State Board of Education, which he had helped establish. His friends thought he had made a great mistake, for the salary of his new job was very low. However, Horace Mann was more interested in doing good than in making money.

As secretary of the State Board of Education, Horace Mann's first big job was to make people want to improve their public schools. He knew that they would never spend money on training better teachers and building better schools unless they saw the need for better public education. He traveled all over the state making speeches about the need for better schools to groups of business people, farmers, and factory workers. In addition, he wrote a long report on the condition of schools in Massachusetts during

Horace Mann asked for better schools. He showed people how the public schools could be improved.

each of the twelve years that he held this job. In these reports, he also discussed the reasons why public education was important. His speeches and reports were so fine and forceful that they succeeded in arousing people's interest in improving the schools.

The second part of Horace Mann's job was to show people how the schools could be improved. In his yearly reports, he made many suggestions about better buildings and better methods of teaching. These reforms soon spread to other states. One of the important things Horace Mann did was to establish the first state teacher-training school in the United States. Before long, there were many such schools in the country.

Although Horace Mann entered politics again in 1848, he spent his last years as a teacher. He served two terms in the United States House of Representatives, and was nominated for governor of Massachusetts. He was defeated in the election, however, and became president of Antioch College at Yellow Springs, Ohio.

Horace Mann's own words are engraved on the monument which marks his grave. "Be ashamed to die until you have won some victory for humanity." This great American's victory was better education for our nation's children.

Antioch College in Ohio. Horace Mann became the first president of this college in 1853.

Clara Barton founded the American Red Cross. She devoted her life to helping other people.

Chapter 11
Clara Barton
1821-1912

Little Clara Barton tiptoed softly into her brother David's room. Gently, she felt his forehead to see if his fever had gone down. Then she filled a glass with cold water and carefully measured out a teaspoonful of medicine. Three months earlier, David had been badly hurt when he fell from the roof of a barn. Since then, Clara had been his devoted nurse.

Clara enjoyed helping other people. Perhaps this was one reason why everyone on the big Barton farm loved her so much. She was

Clara Barton nursed her brother when he was badly hurt. When helping others she forgot her shyness.

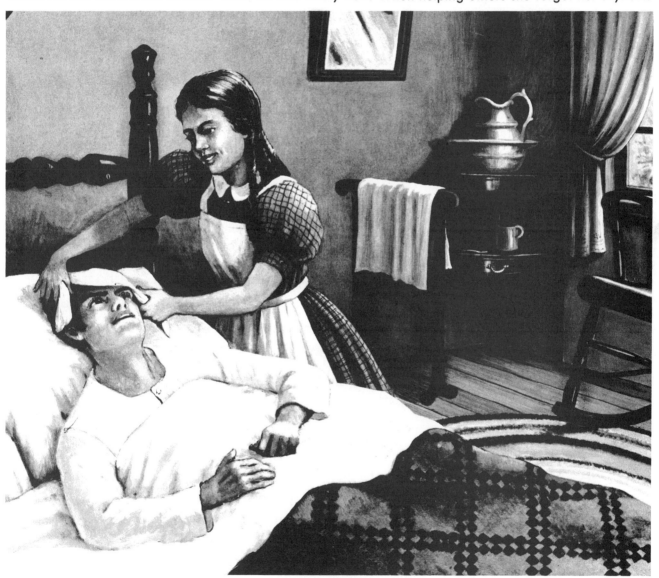

the favorite of all her older brothers and sisters. When she was only three, Sally and Dorothy taught her to read and spell. Before she was four, Stephen carried her on his shoulders to school. By the time she was five, David was teaching her to ride horseback fearlessly, and to play ball as well as a boy.

Home was the only place where Clara was really happy, for she was very shy. Though galloping on a spirited horse did not frighten her, she was terribly afraid of meeting new people. As she grew older, Clara learned that when she was helping other people she forgot about herself and stopped being shy.

With her mother's encouragement, Clara decided to find some kind of work which would be useful to other people. When she was only fifteen, she began to teach school. She continued this work for eighteen years, until a serious breakdown of her voice made teaching impossible. After resting for a while, she went to work in the United States Patent Office in Washington, D. C.

While Clara Barton was in Washington, the Civil War* broke out. Wounded soldiers began to arrive in the city from the battlefield. Clara and several other women helped to take care of these soldiers' wounds. Then Clara placed an advertisement in a newspaper asking for supplies and money for these men. People sent so much food and clothing that she had to rent a warehouse in which to store these supplies. Then she distributed them to the soldiers.

Clara Barton's greatest work during this war, however, was helping wounded soldiers on the battlefield. She had to receive special permission from the army to go to the places where the fighting was done. Completely forgetting about herself, she risked her own life to help the sick and wounded and to comfort the dying. The grateful soldiers called her "The Angel of the Battlefield."

*See Glossary

After the war was over, Clara went to Switzerland for a much-needed rest. While she was there, some gentlemen visited her and told her of a society called the Red Cross. This organization had been founded to help all wounded soldiers, no matter what country

Clara Barton cared for the wounded. The grateful soldiers called her "The Angel of the Battlefield."

Clara Barton served as the president of the American Red Cross for over twenty years.

they were fighting for. Soon Clara became convinced that the Red Cross should be established in America also.

Clara Barton remained in Europe for four years. During her stay, the German and French people fought each other in a bitter war. Clara helped the Red Cross workers in Europe care for soldiers wounded in this struggle. She also helped to distribute money and supplies to men, women, and children who were left hungry and homeless after the war. Several European leaders honored her with medals, to show their gratitude for her help.

When Miss Barton returned to the United States, she worked hard to establish the Red Cross in our country. After much effort she was successful. In 1882, the United States became a member of the International Red Cross. Clara did not stop with this victory, however. She believed that the Red Cross should help victims of floods, earthquakes, and epidemics,* as well as victims of war. Clara persuaded the American Red Cross to give this kind of help. Soon she was also able to persuade the International Red Cross to give help to victims of peacetime disasters.

Clara Barton served as president of the American Red Cross for more than twenty years. Today, this great organization is a living memorial to the woman who forgot about herself in helping others.

A Red Cross worker. The Red Cross helps the victims of wars, floods, and other disasters.

Jane Addams devoted much of her life to helping the poor. She also worked for world peace.

Chapter 12
Jane Addams
1860-1935

Have you ever seen the slums of a great city? Tumble-down houses are crowded along narrow streets. Ragged children play on the sidewalks. Dirt and flies seem to be everywhere. If you know of such places, you will be interested in learning about Jane Addams. This fine American woman spent much of her life helping people who lived in city slums.

Jane Addams was born into a well-to-do Quaker* family in Cedarville, Illinois. When Jane was two years old, her mother died. Jane's father loved her dearly, however, and he took good care of her. Jane was very young when her father took her with him on a business trip to a mill. In the slum section near the factory, Jane saw poor people and tumble-down houses for the first time in her life. She asked her father why people lived like that. He explained their poverty as best he could.

"When I grow up," said Jane, "I am going to build a great, big house and live right by horrid houses like these. Then I will let the people come in to see me for help." Her father little dreamed how well she would keep her promise.

*See Glossary

Children in a slum district. As a girl, Jane Addams decided to help needy people.

Charles J. Hull house in Chicago was purchased by Jane Addams for use as a settlement house.

Jane also planned to be a doctor when she grew up, but this dream did not come true. After graduating from Rockford College in 1881, she entered medical school. However, the next year she became ill and had to leave. To regain her health, she visited Europe. The poverty she saw in the large cities there impressed her more than any of the beautiful, historic places she visited. In London, she stayed for a while at a house much like the one she had wanted ever since she was a girl. She decided to carry out her childhood plan after her return to America.

In 1889, Jane bought a large, brick house in a poor, shabby neighborhood in Chicago. It was called Hull House, after Charles J. Hull who had built it. When Jane Addams moved into this building, she began to fulfill her dream of helping the poor. Hull House became the first settlement house in the Midwest.

Gradually, the poor people Jane wanted so much to help began to come to Hull House. Here they found food, medical care, fun, and classes in many subjects. People of different races and nationalities came together and learned from one another. The comfort and warm friendliness of this big house welcomed everyone. Soon other people began to offer money and hours of free work to help keep Hull House a place of comfort and a refuge for the poor. So many people came to Hull House that new buildings and additions were required. Eventually, Hull House covered a whole city block.

In 1963, the Hull House property was sold to the city of Chicago for the Chicago campus of the University of Illinois. All of the buildings were torn down except for the original mansion that had

Jane Addams told stories to children. People of all ages came to Hull House for help.

been purchased by Jane Addams. This building has been restored on the campus and serves as a museum.

Today, the work begun by Jane Addams is carried on by the Hull House Association. This organization maintains about thirty centers that provide special help to different groups of people. Some centers help teenagers who have trouble in school. Others provide day care for children, food for old people, or first-aid care for people who are waiting for an ambulance to arrive. One of the centers has a program called "Grandma Please," for children whose parents are at work when they come home from school. These children can telephone the "Grandma Please" number and talk to an adult if they need help of any kind.

A peace rally. Jane Addams helped found an international peace organization.

Checking blood pressure at a Hull House Association first-aid center. Today, Jane Addams' work is being carried on in centers run by the Hull House Association.

Although she devoted most of her life to the work at Hull House, Jane Addams helped people in many other ways as well. In Chicago, she helped improve working conditions in factories. She was inspector of that city's streets and alleys for three years. Through her help, the first Juvenile Court in the world was established in Chicago. People of many countries listened to her speak on such problems as public health, child labor, and unemployment. Many others read the articles and books she wrote about these problems.

During her life, Jane Addams worked very hard to help bring peace to the world. In 1915, she helped found an international peace organization, and served as its president for many years. The Nobel Peace Prize* was awarded to her in 1931. President Theodore Roosevelt once called her "America's most useful citizen."

Samuel Clemens wrote under the name "Mark Twain." Many of his stories describe his own experiences.

Chapter 13
Samuel Clemens – "Mark Twain"
1835-1910

In a tiny cabin near Silver City, Nevada, twenty-six-year-old Sam Clemens and his three companions huddled close together to keep warm. A great storm was raging over the Sierra Nevada mountains on this spring day in 1862. The howling wind pulled at the piece of canvas that was stretched across the low log walls of the cabin to form a roof. A cold and hungry cow, walking along a narrow path above the cabin, poked her nose into a hole in one corner of the canvas. Suddenly she slipped. Down she tumbled through the flimsy roof, bringing with her a great shower of ice and snow. Sam and his startled friends scrambled to their feet. Together they pulled and shoved until they got the struggling animal outside.

This was not the first accident that had happened to Sam Clemens since he had left St. Louis, Missouri, to come West the summer before. One time his campfire went out of control and burned up the trees on his timber claim. His dreams of finding glittering masses of silver in the Nevada mining region had not come true. To make matters worse, here he was — snowed in! Sam took out his notebook and began to write. When something bothered him, he often wrote it down. Somehow it helped him to think more clearly. This rugged young man was to become one of America's best-loved authors.

Sam Clemens had many unusual experiences in a Nevada mining camp.

Sam Clemens had not been trained as a writer. He just wrote about the people he met and the things that happened to him. In some of his descriptions, he exaggerated a little or changed the facts somewhat. This made his writing even more humorous and colorful. He painted such vivid word pictures that his stories came to life for other people.

Sam's adventures in the Nevada mining camps gave him much to write about. He sent several of his stories to the *Territorial Enterprise*, a newspaper in nearby Virginia City. The editor of the paper liked them so well that Sam was given a regular job as a reporter. Instead of using his own name, he signed his work "Mark Twain," a pen name which he used for the rest of his life. His stories became so popular that newspapers in other parts of the country also printed them. Several years later, Sam put stories about many of his experiences in the West into a book called *Roughing It*. People still enjoy Sam's humorous descriptions of life in the western territories.

Sam's love of adventure constantly led him to new experiences. In a few years he left Virginia City and took a job with a large newspaper in San Francisco. It was not long before another newspaper sent him to other countries as a foreign correspondent.* Many of the unusual experiences he had on his travels are humorously recorded in his book *The Innocents Abroad*.

In addition to writing about his adventures as a man, Sam Clemens wrote about his childhood experiences. Many of the characters and incidents in his books *The Adventures of Tom Sawyer* and *The Adventures of Huckleberry Finn* are based on people he knew and things that happened to him as a boy in Hannibal, Missouri. A great limestone cave like the one in *Tom Sawyer* really exists near Hannibal. Sam actually did witness a murder, and

*See Glossary

108

A movie scene of Sam Clemens writing. The people he wrote about seemed real and lifelike.

testified to it in court, as Tom does in the book. A boy very much like Huckleberry Finn lived in a tumble-down shack near Sam Clemens' own childhood home. Most important of all, as a boy Sam felt the same way the boys do in parts of his books. Because he could remember and write down how boys feel about things, Sam Clemens was able to make his characters as real as living people.

In his writings, Sam Clemens also used many of his experiences as a steamboat pilot on the Mississippi River. When he took this job at the age of twenty-one, the Mississippi was America's busiest water highway. Beautiful, white steamboats carried passengers from port to port along the river. Tied beside them at the river wharves were dirty freighters piled high with bales of cotton and kegs of whiskey. Dozens of black slaves loaded and unloaded the boats. Many slaves were bought and sold at the docks, along with cattle, horses, and other cargo. These scenes so touched Sam's heart that he wrote about them years later. Though the days of steamboating on the Mississippi are gone forever, we can relive this colorful time in our country's past in his books *Huckleberry Finn* and *Life on the Mississippi.* Many of the people Sam Clemens describes in Huck's trip down the river with a runaway slave are real persons that Sam himself met in his own steamboating days. Thanks to Mark Twain's books, this part of America's story will live forever.

Not all of Sam Clemens' writings are about his own experiences. He enjoyed reading the works of other great authors, especially those about heroes of the past. He included real and imaginary people of earlier times in some of his own writings. When he lived in Hartford, Connecticut, he wrote *A Connecticut Yankee in King Arthur's Court.* In this story, Mark Twain takes us back in time for an imaginary visit to the village of Camelot.* In his book *Personal Recollections of Joan of Arc,* he tells the story of the brave, young French girl who led her nation's armies against the English in 1429-1430. The adventures of a young prince and a poor boy in England about four hundred years ago are described in Clemens' story *The Prince and the Pauper.*

Sam Clemens could entertain people as well with his speeches as he could with books. His slow drawl and good sense of humor

Watching a steamboat on the Mississippi River. Some of Samuel Clemens' writings tell about his experiences as a steamboat pilot on the Mississippi.

made him so popular that he was invited to lecture in many places. He enjoyed doing this, because it gave him a chance to find out what kinds of jokes and stories people liked best.

Though Sam Clemens made many humorous speeches, we remember him best for his stories about the West and about life along the Mississippi. This great American's love of adventure helped him to learn a great deal about the America of his day. His interest in people and his sense of humor helped him appreciate and understand the things he saw. He was able to write about his experiences and the times in which he lived better than anyone else.

Sam Clemens at home. This author's books help us to relive a colorful time in our country's past.

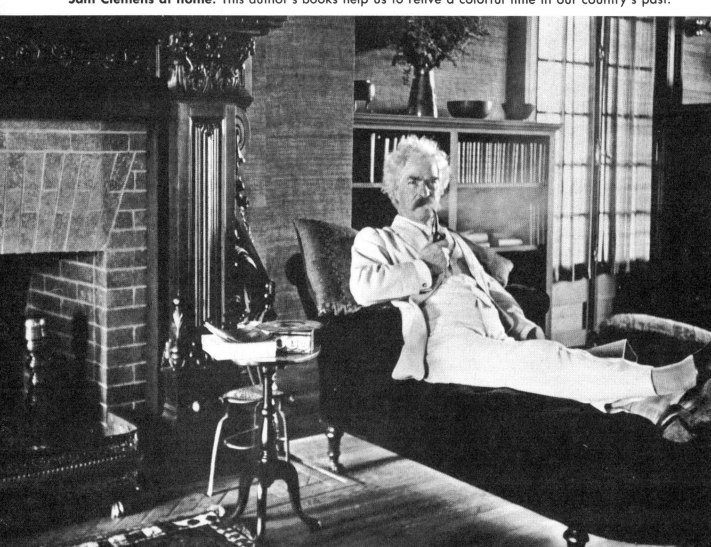

An advertisement. Mark Twain was invited to many communities to make humorous speeches.

John James Audubon was an artist and a naturalist.* He painted true-to-life pictures of American birds.

Chapter 14
John James Audubon
1785-1851

In a sunny meadow just outside the city of Nantes, France, young John James Audubon crouched silently behind a large, gray stone. Three feet away from him in the grass was a nest of scrawny baby larks. The boy watched breathlessly as their mother fluttered down to feed them. John James should have been at

*See Glossary

114

Mourning doves. The birds in Audubon's pictures look so real that they almost seem alive.

home studying mathematics. His father, a French sea captain, thought that schoolwork was much more important than wandering through the fields. What Captain Audubon did not realize was that his son was really studying very hard when he took these trips. He was learning more about his favorite subject, nature.

Although John James and his father did not agree on the importance of nature study, they were alike in other ways. As a young sea captain, the elder Audubon had loved adventure. His travels had taken him to far-off America. In fact, it was there that John James had been born. The boy had his father's love of high adventure.

Young Audubon's chance for adventure came when he was seventeen years old. His father sent him to America to look after some property he owned at Mill Grove, Pennsylvania. John James

Sketching a bird. After he came to America, young Audubon studied the many strange birds he saw.

was very happy at Mill Grove. Much of his time there was spent exploring the countryside, and studying the strange birds he found. He painted many beautiful, true-to-life pictures of them.

As his collection of paintings grew, Audubon began to dream of writing and illustrating a book about American birds. Such a book would mean a great deal of hard work. It would require traveling all over the vast land of America. However, this thought did not frighten adventuresome young Audubon at all.

While he was at Mill Grove, Audubon met and married a lovely girl named Lucy Bakewell. Lucy was proud of her husband's interest in nature and his wonderful skill in drawing birds. She shared his dream of a great book about American birds. Even though it meant that he would be away from home much of the time, she encouraged him to travel in search of birds.

Audubon found it very difficult to make a living for Lucy and their two sons. For a while he ran a general store in Louisville, Kentucky. His store was not very successful, so he moved to another town. However, Audubon was a naturalist* and artist, not a businessman. Finally, he decided to devote all his time to preparing his book. In between his nature trips he earned money by giving dancing and fencing lessons and by drawing portraits. Lucy also worked. She did not complain about their poverty, because she felt it was important for her husband to finish his great book.

When he was forty-one, Audubon was ready to publish his book, *Birds of America.* Though he had completed more than four hundred beautiful paintings, no American publisher was interested in his work. He left for England to see if he could find a publisher there. The English scientists and authors who saw his paintings were very impressed. Before long an English publisher accepted his work. Audubon's long years of poverty were over.

Shoveler ducks. Audubon's pictures show American birds in their natural surroundings.

Another man might have been content with this success. Audubon's work, however, had just started. Before long, he returned to America to search for more birds. He traveled from the swamps of Florida to the cold, snowy coast of Labrador. Some of these trips were difficult and dangerous. Fierce northern storms battered the ship that carried him to Labrador. Clouds of mosquitoes sometimes prevented him from sleeping. However, Audubon gave little thought to his own comfort or safety. He was busy making it possible for other people to share in the rare wonders of nature that he found in these remote places.

Some of the birds which Audubon painted no longer exist. Careless hunters killed them in such large numbers that there are none left. We would have even fewer birds today if, in 1886, a group of Americans had not formed a club to protect our country's wildlife. They called their organization the Audubon Society, in honor of the great American who spent his life studying nature. The Audubon Society has encouraged our government to pass important conservation laws. It has also helped many people enjoy the wonders of nature, just as Audubon did long ago.

American hare. Audubon also painted pictures of American animals.

Thomas A. Edison brought much comfort and pleasure into our lives through his many inventions.

Chapter 15
Thomas A. Edison
1847-1931

One day more than one hundred years ago, a boy walked sadly away from a little, white schoolhouse in Port Huron, Michigan. His teacher had said that he was addlebrained and should not stay in school. This boy later became one of the greatest inventors the world has ever known. His name was Thomas Alva Edison.

Young Al Edison was different from most boys his age. He wanted to know the "why" of everything. His curiosity, ambition, and high intelligence led him in a constant search for new knowledge. Before he was ten years old, he had read many science and history books written for adults. He had also set up a chemical laboratory in the basement of his home.

At the age of twelve, Al decided to become a businessman. He got a job selling newspapers and candy on a train that ran from Port Huron to Detroit. Soon he was selling fresh vegetables and fruits at the stations in both towns. Later, he printed a newspaper in the baggage car of the train, and sold the copies to

A laboratory on wheels. Young Edison set up a laboratory in the train on which he sold papers.

passengers. He found so many ways to increase business that he earned more money than some grown men of that time.

Edison spent most of his money on books and equipment for the "laboratory on wheels" that he had set up in the train's baggage car. One day a chemical fell to the floor of this rolling laboratory. It burst into flames and set the car on fire. The conductor was so angry that he threw Edison, his printing press, and his laboratory equipment off the train for good.

As a young man, Thomas Edison earned his living by working as a telegraph operator.

Edison's first practical invention was a machine that printed stock market prices on paper tape.

This accident started the young man of fifteen on a career as a telegraph operator. He had learned Morse* code during the years he worked on the train. For the next few years, he moved from place to place, working as a telegraph operator. His great ability made other people respect and admire him. As usual, however, he was not content just to work at his job. He also studied, made improvements in the telegraph, and carried out experiments.

By 1869 Edison had decided to become a full-time inventor, even though he had no important inventions. He gave up his job as a telegraph operator, and went to New York City. There,

*See Glossary

123

Edison improved a special telegraph machine that was used to send stock market prices to brokers'* offices. He sold the rights to the patents* on this machine for $40,000. This was the first invention for which he was paid. Edison was only twenty-two years old at this time.

In the years that followed, Edison became famous for his remarkable discoveries and inventions. From his first small workshop in Newark, New Jersey, Edison moved to a larger laboratory

Edison invented an electric light after months of experiments in his laboratory at Menlo Park.

Edison's first light bulb. Electric lights were much more convenient than candles or lamps.

in Menlo Park. In 1887 he moved to a huge laboratory in West Orange, where he employed hundreds of workers.

This great man once said, "Genius is two per cent inspiration and ninety-eight per cent perspiration." He often worked eighteen hours a day in his laboratory. His hard work and his interest in new ideas helped him to patent more than a thousand inventions in his lifetime. Perhaps the most important of these was a practical electric light. Among his other inventions were a new kind of storage battery, a typewriter, and a dictating machine. He improved both the telephone and telegraph. Edison invented "talking pictures" by combining two of his greatest inventions — the phonograph and the motion picture camera.

The little boy who failed in school grew up to be one of our great Americans. He brought more comfort and pleasure into our daily lives than perhaps any other inventor in history.

Listening to the phonograph. This was one of more than a thousand inventions patented* by Edison.

Henry Ford made it possible for millions of Americans to own good, low-cost automobiles.

Chapter 16
Henry Ford
1863-1947

The next time you drive down a great highway streaming with sleek, powerful automobiles, think of Henry Ford. This man helped change not only the way America looked, but also the way people lived.

From the time he was a small boy on his father's farm, Henry was interested in machines. His father hoped that he would become a farmer. However, the only thing about the farm that

Henry liked was the farm machinery. He kept his father's machinery repaired, and even worked on the neighbors' clocks and farm machines in his spare time.

When he was sixteen, Henry left the farm and walked to the nearby city of Detroit, Michigan. His first job was as an apprentice* in a machine shop. Later, he worked in engine shops where he learned to build and repair steam engines. These jobs gave him the training he needed to begin experiments on an automobile.

*See Glossary

Ford built his first automobile in a workshop behind his home. He finished it in 1896.

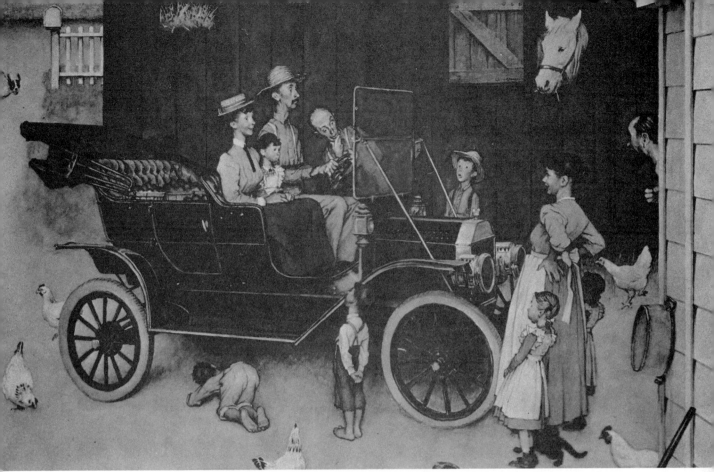

Henry Ford's "horseless carriage." By 1899, Ford had built three different automobiles.

It was to be many years, however, before Henry Ford could devote all his time to experiments. He worked at different jobs to earn a living. At twenty-four he left his job as machinist and operated a sawmill near his father's farm. Later, he returned to Detroit and worked for the Edison Illuminating Company.

No matter what job he had, Henry's real work went on at home. While working for the Edison Company in Detroit he set up a workshop in a shed behind his house. Here, he built his first "horseless carriage."

Late one night in 1896 the little car was ready to run. However, Ford discovered that he couldn't get it out of the workshop. The door was too small. This difficulty did not stop him for long, however. He cut a hole in the workshop wall and drove his car right through it into the street and around the block.

In an early Ford factory. Ford produced millions of low-priced cars by improving methods of working.

Ford drove the car often after this first trial run. How everybody stared at the strange vehicle! It had a boxlike body, bicycle wheels, and a lever to steer with. People laughed when he got out and turned the car around by hand. The little car could not go backward because it had no reverse gear.

Henry Ford was not the first man to build a "horseless carriage." Automobiles were already being sold in the United States and Europe. However, they were made by hand, a few at a time, and were very expensive. Ford's ambition was to build cars so cheaply

130

that people with small incomes could afford to buy them. Most business people laughed at this idea. They thought the automobile would always be a "rich man's toy."

Ford proved that they were wrong. In 1903 he opened a small automobile factory. Within twenty years he was producing cars at such a low cost that many people could afford to buy them. Many thousands of each part were made in Ford's factory. The frames were placed on a moving belt that carried them along a row of workers. As each frame came by, one man put on a wheel, another the steering wheel, and so forth. When the cars reached the end of this "assembly line," they were ready to be driven away. This method of manufacturing is called "mass production." By 1925, mass production methods made it possible for Ford to

Ford shared some of his profits with his workers. He also shortened working hours.

THE WEATHER—
Monday night, cloudy; Tuesday, unsettled, probably snow and rising temperatures; winds moderate northerly, becoming northerly.

THE DETROIT JOURNAL

LAST EDITION

FORTY-FIRST YEAR.

DETROIT, MICHIGAN, MONDAY, JANUARY 5, 1914.

PRICE: Detroit and Suburbs—One cent on street and news stands. 3 cents per week delivered. Elsewhere—two cents.

HENRY FORD GIVES $10,000,000 IN 1914 PROFITS TO HIS EMPLOYES

TEN MILLION FORD PROFITS TO MEN

DETAILS OF THE WORLD'S GREATEST PROFIT-SHARING SCHEME SEE REGULAR PAGE 1.

Motor Kings Who Share Profits With Workers

HENRY FORD.

JAMES COUZENS.

"It is our belief that social justice begins at home," said the vice-president of the Ford Co.

DOUBLES PAY OF 25,000 IN AUTO WORKS

Motor King and Couzens Launch World's Biggest Profit Sharing Scheme as "Act of Social Justice" and for Sake of Idle.

GRANT EIGHT-HOUR DAY AT $5 WAGE

Two Shifts of Nine Hours Changed to Three of Eight, 4,000 Unemployed to Be Taken In—Jobs on Farms Arranged During Slack Season.

The Ford Motor Co. will give to its employes during the year of 1914 the sum of $10,000,000 in addition to their wages.

This will not be a wage increase, but a distribution of profits. It will be added, however, semi-monthly, to the pay envelopes of the men. In 1915, the distribution might be more or less than $10,000,000, dependent on business conditions.

A minimum wage of $5 a day will be established by the addition of the profit distribution to wages. The present minimum wage in the great motor car factory is $2.34. From next Monday to the end of the year, even the lowliest laborer and the man who merely sweeps the floors, will get at least $5 a day.

Further, the 8-hour day is instituted. At present the Ford factory has two 9-hour shifts. It now will install three 8-hour shifts, the factory working continuously.

Between 25,000 and 30,000 men will benefit greatly by the profit distribution.

Fifteen thousand of them now work in the huge factory out Woodward avenue. Four thousand more men are to be hired there during the present month and will come under the profit-sharing plan. The others who will share in the rich division number 7,000 to 8,000 and are scattered all over the world, working in Ford branches in Canada, Mexico, South America,

Every male Ford employe 22 years old will share at once in the distribution. About 10 per cent of the employes in the factory here are women, engaged in the electrical department or in office work, and boys between 18 and 22. The women will not share in the distribution, not being considered the economic factors that men workers are, but they will get substantial wage boosts instead. Of the boys between 18 and 22, those who support their families or have others dependent on their earnings, will be included with their older fellow workers in the profit-sharing.

No man will be discharged from the Ford employ except for unfaithfulness or proved inefficiency. Foremen will not be able to discharge employes. The employe will be given chances to make good in one department after another until the proper niche for him is found or his complete inefficiency is established.

If the factory is compelled to shut down for a time, things will be arranged to have the lay-off period come in the summer time, when farmers are calling for harvest hands and the men laid off will have a chance to step out of the factory and work for a time in the fields.

The plan of profit distribution is one of social justice, the Ford Co. declares. The extra money to the employe will not come out of the public, as prices of cars will not be raised, but will be lowered when possible. The money will be diverted from the stockholders to the workingmen.

The Ford Co.'s financial statement as of Sept. 30, 1912, showed assets of $20,815,785.63 and surplus of $14,745,095.57. One year later, Sept. 30, 1913, it showed assets of $35,033,919.58 and surplus of $28,124,172.66.

The profit sharing plan of the Ford Motor Co., whereby its employes will divide $10,000,000 in the present year, was announced to the newspapers of the city by Henry Ford, president, and James Couzens, vice-president and treasurer, Monday morning.

Seated in Mr. Couzens' office at the plant out Woodward avenue the two motor car men discussed quietly the greatest step ever taken in industrial history. That the details of their plan would startle the whole world did not excite them. Mr. Couzens announced simply that they had decided upon a plan to share their prosperity with their employes, and first of all he wanted the newspaper men to know the details of the idea they had prepared.

Mr. Couzens then read from a statement covering the details, inviting questions on any points that needed elucidation.

UNEMPLOYED AS REASON

Mr. Ford was looking out of the side window of the office when the discussion ended. From the window was a view down Woodward avenue and along part of Manchester avenue to the side of the factory. Three or four hundred men were in the streets and on the sidewalks, some heading for the employment entrance to ask for work, others on the look.

"There's the principal reason for

Instead of waiting until the end of the year to make a distribution of profits among their employes in one lump bonus sum, Mr. Ford and Mr. Couzens have estimated the year's prospective business and have decided upon what they feel will be a safe amount to award the workers. This will be spread over the whole year and paid on the regular semi-monthly pay days.

The factory is now working two shifts of nine hours each. This will be changed to three shifts of eight hours each. The number employed is now about 15,000 and this will be increased by 4,000 or 5,000. The men who now earn $2.34 per day of nine hours will get at least $5 per day of eight hours.

This will apply to every man of 22 years of age or upward without regard to the nature of his employment. In order that the young man from 18 to 22 years of age may be entitled to a share in the profits he must show himself sober, saving, steady, industrious and must satisfy the superintendent and staff that his money will not be wasted in riotous living.

Young men who are supporting families, widowed mothers, younger brothers and sisters will be treated like those over 22.

It is estimated that over $10,000,000 will be thus distributed over and above the regular wages of the men.

"The commonest laborer who sweeps the floor shall receive his pay," said Henry Ford.

WHERE JUSTICE BEGINS

"It is our belief," said Mr. Couzens, "that social justice begins at home. We want those who have helped us to produce this great institution and are helping to maintain it, to share our prosperity. We want them to have present profits and future prospects. Thrift and good service and sobriety all will be encouraged and rewarded."

"If we are obliged," said Mr. Ford, "to lay men off for want of sufficient work at any season we propose to plan our year's work that the lay-off shall be in the summer and not in the winter. We hope to make it easy for the farmers who have hired our men at good wages to send them back to us in the busy seasons. We shall make it our business to get in touch with the farmers and to induce our men to spend their vacation—or rather—for harvest time.

"No man will be discharged for any cause of unfaithfulness or inefficiency. No foreman in the Ford Co. has the power to discharge a man. He may send him out of his department to be made good. The man he thus sends out to try 'libertine house' covering all the departments and is remedially tried in other work until we find the job he is suited for provided he is honestly trying to render good service.

"We are quite sure," said Mr. Couzens, "that we shall still pay handsome dividends to our stockholders and will not settle reasonable amounts for additions and improvements and assembling plants in other parts of the country, and after that it is our hope to be able to do still better by our employes. We want them to be in really partners for our enterprise.

SETS THE PACE

The Ford Motor Co. is capitalized at $2,000,000. Its tremendous outlays in recent years have been marvels of the industrial and financial world. It has paid out in amounts in dividends to the stockholders, held the capital stock of the company, and to its best assorted enormous factory and warehouse buildings. Even the surplus practically doubled in the single year from Sept. 30, 1912, to Sept. 30, 1913.

A comparison of the financial sheets, issued by the company shows the recent growth of Ford Co.

Balance sheet, Sept. 30, 1912.

HENRY FORD GIVES $10,000,000 OF PROFITS TO HIS EMPLOYES

Continued from First Page.

Continued on Page Nine.

produce cars at the rate of four every minute. After Ford proved that this method was successful, manufacturers all over the country began to use it.

Henry Ford surprised the whole country in 1914. He announced that ten million dollars of his company's profits were to be shared with his workers. At the same time he shortened working hours. Other manufacturers said that he was crazy. They were sure that his factory would fail now. However, the huge Ford plant in Dearborn, Michigan, and many other Ford factories throughout the world show how wrong these doubters were.

The Ford Plant at Dearborn, Michigan, is one of the many Ford factories throughout the world.

George Washington Carver was a scientist who helped people live healthier, happier lives.

Chapter 17
George Washington Carver
1865(?)-1943

Professor George Washington Carver held up a handful of tangled string for his students to see. Then he held up some old string that had been untangled. It was wound neatly into a ball, ready to be used. The Professor was trying to help his students understand an important idea. Nature does not make any waste. Some things might seem useless, like the tangled string. But if people use their minds, they can find a way to use everything.

George Washington Carver was a black scientist who spent his life trying to show people how to live healthier, happier lives. One way he did this was by helping people to make better use of their minds. Another was by making useful products out of natural materials that were available to everyone.

George was born on a farm near Diamond Grove, Missouri, during the Civil War. His mother was a slave named Mary, who belonged to a couple named Moses and Susan Carver. Moses and Susan treated Mary more like a family member than a slave. When George was a baby, he and Mary were kidnapped by people who stole slaves. A neighbor found George and brought him back to the Carvers. Mary was never found, so the Carvers took George and his brother Jim into their home and brought them up like their own children.

Susan and Moses Carver realized very early that George was a special boy. He was not very strong, so he could not work in the fields with Moses and Jim. But he quickly learned all about cooking and other household skills from Susan. George loved nature and spent a great deal of time outdoors. He learned so much about plants that the neighbors called him the "plant doctor."

Young George was full of questions about the world around him. Moses and Susan Carver answered his questions as well as they could, but he wanted to know more. He tried to go to the school in his community and was told that it was not open to black children. The nearest school for blacks was in the town of Neosho, eight miles away. When Moses and Susan Carver thought George was old enough, they let him move there to go to school.

For the next thirty years, George Washington Carver moved from place to place in search of knowledge. In several towns, he stayed with families who let him help with the housework in exchange for food while he went to school. For a while, he stopped school and worked. Finally in 1894, he graduated from Iowa State College of Agriculture and Mechanic Arts.

As a boy, George knew so much about plants that he was called the "plant doctor."

At Tuskegee Institute, Professor Carver went for daily walks to gather plants to show his students. The United States government asked his help in learning about plant diseases.

George Washington Carver won the love and respect of his teachers and fellow students everywhere he went. He continued to study and teach at Iowa State after graduation, and was asked to stay on there and teach. However, he did not accept this offer. An invitation had come to teach at a new school for blacks in Alabama, called Tuskegee Institute. George Washington Carver felt that was where he belonged.

Tuskegee Institute had been started by a black educator named Booker T. Washington. His dream was to help blacks in the South learn the skills that would help them have a better way of life.

Until the Civil War,* most blacks had lived in slavery. Now they were free, but their lives were still very hard. Most of them were farmers who did not own their own land. Their main crop was cotton, which wore out the soil if it was planted year after year. The kind of food they ate did not provide what was needed for good health. They did not know how to improve their lives, for most of them had no education.

George Washington Carver shared Booker T. Washington's dream of helping his people. To show them new and better ways of farming, Professor Carver started an experiment station. Here he tried

*See Glossary

In his laboratory, Professor Carver made useful products out of different natural materials.

out new kinds of crops that would build up the soil and provide a healthy diet. He also developed new kinds of seeds that produced larger crops.

Professor Carver was careful to use methods that were cheap and easy enough for poor farmers to copy. He wrote bulletins* that explained scientific farming methods in words that were easy for ordinary people to understand. These bulletins also included recipes for cooking new and healthful kinds of meals.

George Washington Carver knew that some farmers could not read his bulletins. He fixed up a demonstration wagon, on which he put farm tools and seeds, and drove this from place to place to show people better ways of farming. He also helped set up special summer classes for farmers at Tuskegee Institute.

Professor Carver believed that people could meet their needs if they would only make good use of the gifts nature gave them. In college, he had studied a kind of science called chemistry. Chemists work in laboratories to break down products into the elements, or basic materials from which they are made. Then they combine these elements to make new products. Tuskegee Institute did not have much money, so George Washington Carver used bottles and jars from the trash dump to make a simple laboratory.

Later, George Washington Carver was able to get better laboratory equipment. He experimented to find ways of making useful products out of natural materials that were available in the South. For example, he learned to make house paint out of clay, and milk out of peanuts. He even made products out of peanut shells.

As time went on, people outside Tuskegee Institute began to learn about George Washington Carver. Letters came to him from all over the world asking his advice on farming problems. The United

Painting. George Washington Carver had studied art at Simpson College when he was a young man.

States Department of Agriculture asked his help in working with plant diseases and other matters. He received medals and other high honors for his discoveries.

As he became more and more famous, Dr. Carver was invited to speak at colleges and other places throughout the United States. Many of his listeners were white people who had never had an opportunity to be around blacks. George Washington Carver helped these people realize that the color of a person's skin is not important. It is the kind of person one is inside that counts.

George Washington Carver never used his fame or discoveries to gain riches for himself. He dressed and lived very simply all his life. Before his death, he used all his life savings to establish the Carver Museum and the George Washington Carver Foundation for Agricultural Research at Tuskegee. Here scientists have continued Dr. Carver's search for ways to help people live healthier, happier lives.

People loved to listen to George Washington Carver. He made speeches to many groups.

Rachel Carson was a scientist and writer who helped to start the environmental* movement.

Chapter 18
Rachel Carson
1907-1964

One winter day in 1958, a slim, blue-eyed woman named Rachel Carson opened a letter from a friend. The friend's name was Olga Owens Huckins. Olga loved nature. She had set aside part of the land she owned in Duxbury, Massachusetts as a place where wild birds could live in safety. In past years, this bird sanctuary* had been filled with singing birds. But this year, it was silent.

*See Glossary

141

Using a microscope. Rachel Carson worked for the United States Fish and Wildlife Service.

The birds had been killed by a poison called DDT. Workers sent by the state government had sprayed DDT all over the countryside to kill mosquitoes. They did not seem to understand that DDT killed birds and animals, too. Olga's letter begged Rachel Carson to find someone in the government who would make the workers stop spraying DDT.

Rachel Carson was a good person to ask for help. She was a well-known scientist who loved nature. For many years, she had worked in a part of the government called the United States Fish and Wildlife Service. She had also written several books. One of these books, *The Sea Around Us,* was so popular that it had been translated into thirty-two languages.

Olga's letter made Rachel Carson write another book, called *Silent Spring*. This was to become one of the most important books to be written in modern times. It made millions of people begin to think about protecting the world that nature has created for us to live in. We call this world our natural environment.* The work that people are doing to protect it is called the environmental movement.

Rachel Carson's childhood helped prepare her for writing this important book. The Carson family lived on a farm near Springdale, Pennsylvania. Rachel's mother had been a school teacher before her children were born. She taught Rachel to love nature. As a child, Rachel spent many hours in the fields and beside streams, learning about birds and insects and flowers.

Rachel grew up on a farm in Pennsylvania. Her mother taught her to love nature.

As a child, Rachel also spent many hours writing. When she was ten years old, she won a prize for an article she wrote for a children's magazine. Rachel thought she would become a writer when she grew up. But she changed her mind and decided to become a scientist after taking a science course called biology in college. Biology is the study of living things.

While she was in college, Rachel spent some time working in a laboratory that studied the living creatures that make their home in the ocean. After college, she went on to get more education about life in the sea. During the summers, she taught science at the university she was attending.

Because she could write well and knew about science, Rachel Carson got a job writing for a series of radio broadcasts about nature. These broadcasts were put on by a part of our country's government called the Bureau of Fisheries. In 1940, this office became part of the United States Fish and Wildlife Service. Its job was the conservation, or taking care, of our nation's birds, fish, and other wild creatures.

Before she went to work for the government, Rachel's father and married sister died. Rachel had to take care of her sister's children and her mother. To earn extra money to support all these people, she began to write science articles for a newspaper and for magazines. One magazine article about the sea was so interesting that Rachel was asked to write a whole book about this subject. The first book she wrote was called *Under the Sea-Wind*. The next was *The Sea Around Us*.

Rachel Carson earned enough money from *The Sea Around Us* to stop working for the government and spend all her time writing. She built a cottage near the ocean, where she could spend summers studying the sea plants and animals along the shore. She also adopted a little grandnephew, and began to teach him about nature, the same way her mother had taught her. She enjoyed working with this little boy so much that she wrote an article called "Help Your Child to Wonder" for a magazine. It was at this happy time that she received her friend Olga's letter about the birds that were being killed by DDT.

Rachel enjoyed studying plants and animals that lived near the edge of the ocean.

Rachel wrote books and articles about nature. Her book *Silent Spring* made people aware that pesticides* were being used in ways that harmed the environment.

At first, Rachel thought she would only write a magazine article telling about the dangers of DDT. But soon she realized the problem was so serious that she needed to write a book. She stopped everything else she was doing and started work on *Silent Spring*.

To get information for *Silent Spring*, Rachel Carson wrote to scientists all over the world. She learned that many other poisons even more dangerous than DDT were being used to kill unwanted insects and weeds. They were being spread over large areas with no attempt to protect harmless plants and animals. People were not being warned about how dangerous these poisons were.

Silent Spring made the companies that manufactured poisons to kill weeds and insects very angry. They made fun of Rachel Carson and tried to prove that she was wrong. But people who read the book did not believe them. Finally President Kennedy formed a group called the President's Science Advisory Committee to find out if what Rachel Carson said was true.

Rachel Carson was very sick at this time, but she came to our nation's lawmaking assembly and told what she knew about pesticides.* The President's Science Advisory Board believed what she said. Laws were passed that helped to make people use dangerous poisons more carefully. More important, people began to realize the importance of protecting nature. Today, people all over the world are trying to take care of the environment, thanks to a brave and loving woman named Rachel Carson.

Rachel Carson helped people realize the importance of protecting nature.

Jonas Salk developed a way to protect people from the terrible disease of polio.*

Chapter 19
Jonas Salk
1914-

It was a hot summer day in 1952. Polio* season had begun. All over the country families waited in fear for the terrible illness to strike without warning. Ambulances lined up at hospitals with hundreds of new polio cases each day. Hospital rooms and hallways were crowded with thousands of new patients. Most of the polio patients were children.

*See Glossary

In Pittsburgh, Pennsylvania, Dr. Jonas Salk worked day and night in his laboratory. He was searching for a way to end the horror of polio. Sometimes he would leave his laboratory and walk through the halls of Municipal Hospital. He would try to comfort children sick with polio. Their cries of pain often brought tears to his kind eyes.

Dr. Salk worked day and night on his experiments. Time after time he met failure. The people working with him sometimes wanted to give up. Dr. Salk inspired them to go on with their important work. His quiet strength and friendly smile encouraged them to keep trying. Dr. Salk could not even think of giving up when children were dying only yards away from his laboratory.

A polio patient. This girl's lungs were paralyzed* by polio. A machine helps her breathe.

Playing checkers. Sometimes a polio patient's arms and legs were paralyzed.

On July 2, 1952, Jonas Salk drove over dusty, country roads to the small town of Leetsdale. He was on his way to conduct a secret experiment. Dr. Salk had finally succeeded in developing a new vaccine* that he believed would work against polio. He was eager to test it for the first time on people.

Dr. Salk entered the cool auditorium of the Watson Home for Crippled Children. He sat down near the end of a long table. On the table were hypodermic* needles and cotton. The air was filled with the whispers and excited laughter of the children who lived at the home. It was an important day. They were going to help Dr. Salk with his experiment.

Many of the children sat in wheelchairs or walked with crutches. "Hi, Dr. Jonas," shouted a small dark-haired boy in a wheelchair. Dr. Salk looked up and smiled broadly. He waved to his young friend.

One by one, Dr. Salk inoculated* each child with his new vaccine. He was very gentle. Few of the children even felt the tiny needle prick their skin. As he worked, Dr. Salk laughed and talked with the children. They all knew and loved him. He was their friend. They knew he wanted to save other children from suffering. Everyone trusted Dr. Salk. He was that kind of person.

Late that night, Dr. Salk bent over a microscope in his laboratory. He studied the tiny blood samples taken from the children at Leetsdale. What he saw excited him very much. The vaccine worked!

Immunizing* against polio. Before Dr. Salk developed the polio vaccine, there was no way to protect people against getting this disease. Thousands of people became crippled or died.

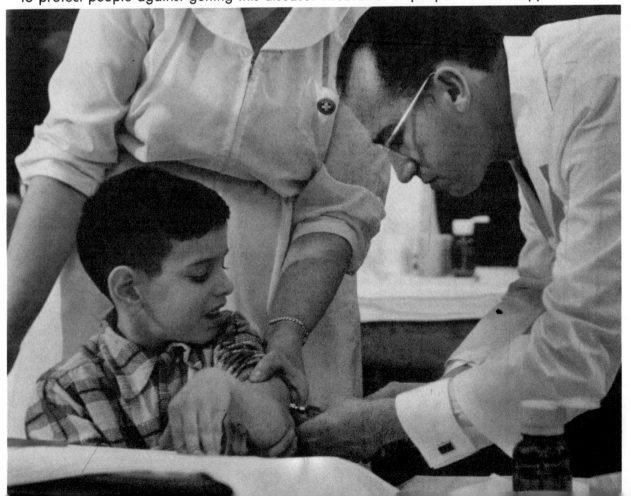

Within a few years, millions of children were being inoculated with the Salk vaccine. Protected by the vaccine, they no longer had to fear that they would get polio. This dread disease had been conquered!

Jonas Salk was the kind of boy you would expect to discover great things. Young Jonas was deeply interested in the world around him. He had a quick mind. He loved to read and to ask questions. He always wanted to know the "why" of things.

Jonas also had a great love for people. He felt compassion and tenderness for people in trouble. He saw much suffering in the neighborhoods of New York City where he lived. Jonas wanted to be able to help people someday.

At New York's City College, Jonas discovered the world of science. He loved to conduct experiments and would spend hours over his microscope. In college, Jonas decided to become a doctor. He wanted to discover new things that would help people and make a better world.

At the New York University School of Medicine, Jonas spent as much time as he could in the laboratory. He wanted to learn about the causes of disease. His teachers liked Jonas. He studied very hard. Sometimes he worked in the laboratory long after everyone else had gone home. Jonas eventually decided he did not want to be the kind of doctor who worked with patients. Instead, he wanted to give his life to research.* He wanted to help discover the causes of sickness.

In 1948, Dr. Salk began his research on polio while at Pittsburgh's Municipal Hospital. A team of assistants worked with him. At that time there was no way to keep people from becoming sick with polio. Doctors were helpless against it. Some medical scientists believed that no vaccine could ever be developed to fight polio.

Others believed that a vaccine of live polio viruses* might be developed. However, this was very dangerous. It would mean giving people the polio virus in the hope that they would develop an immunity* to the disease.

Dr. Jonas Salk worked for four years to develop the Salk vaccine.

Dr. Salk questioned these ideas. He believed that it might be possible to make a vaccine from dead polio viruses that would be both safe and effective against polio. Many scientists laughed at this, but Dr. Salk believed in himself and his idea.

Jonas Salk set up his own laboratory in Pittsburgh to test his idea and to carry out research. He sometimes worked seven days a week, and even twenty-four hours at a time, without rest. His assistants worked equally hard. They were inspired by Dr. Salk's selfless work.

Dr. Salk wanted nothing for himself. He did not care about money. He cared only about people, people in need. He gave his vaccine freely to the world. No one would ever again needlessly suffer the horror of polio. Today, Dr. Jonas Salk is honored by people all over the world for his gift of the Salk vaccine.

Dr. Salk with President Jimmy Carter. In 1977 Jonas Salk received the Presidential Medal of Freedom* at the White House. This is one of the highest honors an American can receive.

GLOSSARY

alcohol. A colorless liquid that affects people's behavior, found in drinks such as beer and whiskey.

amendment (uh MEND ment). A change in, or an addition to, a constitution or a law. See **constitution.**

American Philosophical (fil uh SOF uh kul) **Society.** A society, or club, started by Benjamin Franklin in 1743. He wanted to bring scientists and other educated people in the colonies together. Today, the members of this society include hundreds of well-known scientists from the United States and other countries. See **scientist.**

antislavery. Against slavery. See **slavery.**

apprentice (uh PREN tis). A person who is learning a job by working under the direction of a skilled worker.

bifocal glasses. Eyeglasses with two sections for each eye. The top sections are for looking at things far away. The bottom sections are for looking at things close up. Before Benjamin Franklin invented bifocal glasses, many persons had to use two different pairs of glasses.

bond. A paper given by a government or company to a lender from whom it borrows money. The paper states that the borrower will pay the money back with interest, or additional money, on a certain date.

boycott. The action of a group of people who refuse to do business with a particular person, company, or nation.

broker. A person who buys and sells stocks and bonds for other people. See **stock** and **bond.**

bulletin. A paper or pamphlet that gives information.

Camelot. A legendary place on the island of Great Britain where King Arthur is said to have had his palace and court.

civil rights. The rights and freedoms that belong to a person as a member of a community, a state, or a country. There are many different civil rights. Among them are the right to speak freely and to attend the church of one's choice. Others are the right to own property, the right to a fair trial, and the right to get a job or a place to live. Sometimes the right to vote is also thought of as a civil right.

Civil War, 1861-1865. Also called the War Between the States. This unhappy struggle began after many of the southern states decided to leave the Union. The northern states were determined to prevent this. After many bloody battles, the main Confederate forces surrendered on April 9, 1865. See **Union** and **Confederate States of America.**

colonial. Refers to a certain period of time in the history of the United States. The colonial period began when the first European colonies were started in America. It lasted until the thirteen British colonies became the United States in 1776.

colony. A settlement outside the country that controls it. In American history, it usually means any one of thirteen British colonies along the Atlantic coast. These colonies were started by people from Europe in the 1600's and 1700's. Later, the thirteen colonies became the United States.

Confederate States of America. The eleven southern states that left, or seceded from, the United States in 1860 and 1861.

Congress. A group of people who are elected to make the laws for the United States. Congress is made up of two parts, or houses. These are the Senate and the House of Representatives.

conservation. Saving or protecting something so it will not be wasted. For example, forests, soil, and water need to be conserved.

constitution. A set of rules telling how a country or a state is supposed to be governed. When this word is written with a capital "C," it usually means the Constitution of the United States. Our Constitution was written in 1787. It has been in use ever since.

Continental Congress. A meeting of leaders from the colonies in America that later joined together to form the United States. There were two Continental Congresses. The First Continental Congress met in 1774 to discuss the quarrel between the colonies and Great Britain. The second Continental Congress met in 1775, soon after the Revolutionary War began. On July 4, 1776, it approved the Declaration of Independence. For several years after this, the Second Continental Congress served as the government of the United States. See **Revolutionary War.**

correspondent. A person who writes for newspapers or magazines, usually from another city, state, or country.

debate. A public discussion or argument about some important question. In a debate, there are two or more persons who give different points of view.

Declaration of Independence. A public statement made by leaders of the American colonies on July 4, 1776. This statement said that the colonies were independent, or free, of Great Britain.

democracy. A country in which people govern themselves. The people choose their leaders and make decisions by majority vote.

Democrat. A member of the Democratic Party. This is one of the two main political parties in our country. The other is the Republican Party. See **political.**

democratic. Refers to a country in which the people choose their leaders and make decisions by voting. See **democracy.**

demonstrate. To show or explain. Sometimes, to meet with other people in public to show one's feelings about something.

demonstration. A march or other public action taken by a group of people to show their feelings about something.

depression. A time when many people are out of work and businesses are not able to make much money.

edited. Corrected, or prepared to be published.

elect. To choose a person for a job by voting. Usually the person who receives the most votes gets the job.

election. The choosing of someone for a job or a government office by voting.

Emancipation (ee man sih PAYshun) **Proclamation.** A public statement made by President Lincoln on January 1, 1863. This proclamation freed the slaves in the parts of the Confederacy that were still fighting against the Union. See **Civil War** and **Confederate States of America.**

environment. All of the objects and conditions that surround living creatures and influence their development. The environment of human beings includes such things as air, sunlight, water, rocks, plants, and animals.

environmental movement. The joint efforts of many people to take care of the environment. See **environment.**

epidemic (eh pih DEM ik). An outbreak of a disease. In an epidemic, many people have the same disease at the same time.

experiment. A test planned to discover facts about nature or to help decide whether or not something is true. Also, a test to see if a new idea will work.

Franklin stove. An iron stove for heating a room. It looks something like an open fireplace, but it is not built into a wall. For this reason, it spreads heat in all directions.

French and Indian War, 1754-1763. A war in North America. In this war, Great Britain and its American colonies defeated the French. Indians fought on both sides. As a result of the war, Great Britain took over most of the land that the French had owned in North America.

grant. A gift of money, often given by a school to a student.

Great Britain. A large island that lies off the western coast of Europe. It is made up of three parts–England, Scotland, and Wales. Long ago, these were three countries with different rulers. Wales was joined to England during the 1500's. Then, in 1707, England and Wales were united with Scotland to form the kingdom of Great Britain. The ruler of Great Britain also ruled the British colonies in America. Later, the northern part of Ireland became part of the kingdom of Great Britain. Today, the official name for this country is "The United Kingdom of Great Britain and Northern Ireland."

Henry, Patrick, 1736-1799. American statesman and orator at the time of the Revolutionary War. He inspired many people by his bold speeches against the British.

hypodermic (hi puh DER mik) **needle.** A hollow needle used to put medicine or vaccine under a person's skin. See **vaccine.**

immunity (im MUNE ih tee). The ability to keep from getting a certain disease. For example, a person who has had chicken pox usually will not get that disease again. We say that this person has an immunity to chicken pox.

immunizing (IM u nize ing). Protecting against a disease or a poison.

inaugural (in AW gyur ul). Refers to the beginning of a person's new term of office. May also refer to the speech given by such a person.

inaugural speech. A formal speech or statement made by a person at the beginning of his or her term of office. See **inauguration.**

inauguration (in aw gyur RAY shun). The official installation of a person in office, such as the inauguration of a president.

inoculate (in AHK yu late). To give a person a mild form of a disease by a shot of dead or weakened germs. Inoculation keeps the person from getting a more serious form of the disease.

lightning rod. A metal rod set up on a building or a ship. Its purpose is to lead lightning from the sky into the ground or the water. This keeps the lightning from starting a fire or doing other damage.

Louisiana Purchase. The purchase of a vast territory by the United States from France in 1803. For about 15 million dollars, the United States bought almost a million square miles of land from the Mississippi River to the Rocky Mountains.

minister. A person sent by the government to the government of a foreign country to conduct official business. Also, a person whose job it is to preach, lead services, and do other religious tasks in a church.

Morse code. A system invented by Samuel Morse for sending messages by telegraph. To send telegraph messages by Morse code, letters of the alphabet and numerals are represented by different combinations of short and long sounds.

naturalist. A person trained in the study of nature, especially plants or animals.

natural resources. Useful things found in nature, such as soil, water, trees, and minerals.

New England. An area in the northeastern part of our country. Four of the thirteen British colonies along the Atlantic coast were in New England. (See **colony.**) These were Massachusetts, New Hampshire, Connecticut, and Rhode Island. Today, New England includes these four states plus Maine and Vermont.

New York State Senate. See **senate.**

Nobel (no BELL) **Peace Prize.** A prize given almost every year to a person who has worked for peaceful solutions to important problems.

overseer. A person who directs other workers.

paralyzed (PARE uh lized). Made unable to move.

patent (PAT ent). An official paper issued by the government, giving an inventor control of the manufacture and sale of the invention for a certain number of years.

pesticides (PES tih sides). Substances that kill insects, mice, and other unwanted living things.

plantation. A large farm where a crop such as cotton, tobacco, or sugarcane is raised. The workers usually live on the plantation.

polio. A short form of the word poliomyelitis. This is a serious disease that causes fever and weakness of the muscles. Some people die from polio and some become lame.

political. Having to do with citizens or government.

political district. One of the parts into which a city, county, state, or territory is divided for elections.

politics. The management of public affairs as a profession. The science of government.

prejudice (PREJ uh dis). An opinion that is formed without knowing all the facts. The dislike for a person just because he or she belongs to a different group is a common kind of prejudice.

Presidential Medal of Freedom. An important award given to citizens who are not members of our armed forces.

Quaker (KWAY ker). A member of a religious group called the Society of Friends. This group was started in England by George Fox about 1650.

research. A careful search for facts or truth about a subject.

reservation. An area of land owned by the government and set aside for some special use. Especially, an area set aside for use by Indians.

Revolutionary War, 1775-1783. A war between Great Britain and thirteen British colonies in America. The colonies won the war and became states in a new country. This was the United States.

sanctuary (SANK chu air ee). A place of protection. Also a part of a church where worship services are held.

scientist. An expert in some branch of science. A scientist makes an orderly study of natural laws and facts about nature.

Second Continental Congress. See **Continental Congress.**

seminary. A school or college where students are trained to be religious leaders, such as ministers.

senate. A lawmaking body of a national or state government.

slavery. The custom of owning slaves.

slum. A crowded, run-down part of a city or town. Most of the people who live in slums are very poor.

Stamp Act. A law passed by the British Parliament in 1765, which required all American documents, including newspapers, to be printed on stamped paper purchased from the British government.

stock. A share of ownership in a company. The price of stocks changes frequently.

survey. To determine the exact location and extent of a land area.

temperance groups. Groups that were organized to stop people from drinking beer and other drinks that contain alcohol.

Union. The United States of America. During the Civil War, the northern states were called the Union. See **Civil War.**

United Nations. An organization of countries from all over the world. It was started in 1945 to work for world peace. About 160 countries now belong to the United Nations.

Universal Declaration of Human Rights. A document accepted by the United Nations in 1948 explaining that every person is born free and is equal in dignity and rights. This document was prepared to give people everywhere a standard, or way of measuring, how they treat each other. See **United Nations.**

university. A kind of school that students may attend after finishing high school. A university is made up of several parts called schools or colleges. For example, a university may include schools of law, medicine, and business.

vaccine (VAK seen). The material used to inoculate a person. See **inoculate.**

violence. The use of force to harm someone or to cause damage to something.

virus. Any of certain kinds of germs that cause diseases such as colds and chicken pox.

women's rights. Civil rights for women. See **civil rights.**

World War I, 1914-1918. A war that was fought in many parts of the world. On one side were the Central Powers. These were Germany, Austria-Hungary, Turkey, and Bulgaria. They were defeated by the Allies. These included Great Britain, France, Russia, Japan, the United States, and other countries.

World War II, 1939-1945. A war that was fought in many parts of the world. On one side were the Allies. These included the United States, Great Britain, the Soviet Union, France, and many other countries. On the other side were the Axis Powers, which included Germany, Italy, and Japan. The Allies defeated the Axis Powers.

INDEX